To order, call **1-800-543-0874** and ask for operator BB or fax your order to **1-800-874-1916**, or visit our online catalog at www.nationalunderwriter.com.

PAYMENT INFORMATION

Add shipping & handling charges to all orders as indicated. If your order exceeds total amount listed in chart, call 1-800-543-0874 for shipping & handling charge. Any order of 10 or more items or $250.00 and over will be billed for shipping by actual weight, plus a handling fee. Unconditional 30 day guarantee.

SHIP
(
$20
40
60
80
110
150
200
These
in the L
1-800-54.

MW00423625

The
NATIONAL
UNDERWRITER
Company
PROFESSIONAL PUBLISHING GROUP

The National Underwriter Co. • Orders Dept #2-BB
P.O. Box 14448 • Cincinnati, OH 45250-9786
1-800-543-0874

2-BB

_____ Copies of *Power Netweaving* (#1370000) $32.95

_____ Copies of *Getting It Issued* (#2460002) $29.95

_____ Copies of *From Worksite Marketing to Website Marketing* (#1300004) $29.95

❑ Check enclosed*   ❑ Charge my VISA/MC/AmEx (circle one)   ❑ Bill me

*Make check payable to The National Underwriter Company. Please include the appropriate shipping & handling charges and any applicable sales tax (see charts above).

Card # _____ Exp. Date _____

Signature _____

Name _____Title _____

Company _____

Street Address _____

City _____ State _____ Zip _____

Business Phone (_____) _____ Fax (_____) _____

E-mail_____

The
NATIONAL
UNDERWRITER
Company
PROFESSIONAL PUBLISHING GROUP

The National Underwriter Co. • Orders Dept #2-BB
P.O. Box 14448 • Cincinnati, OH 45250-9786
1-800-543-0874

2-BB

_____ Copies of *Power Netweaving* (#1370000) $32.95

_____ Copies of *Getting It Issued* (#2460002) $29.95

_____ Copies of *From Worksite Marketing to Website Marketing* (#1300004) $29.95

❑ Check enclosed*   ❑ Charge my VISA/MC/AmEx (circle one)   ❑ Bill me

*Make check payable to The National Underwriter Company. Please include the appropriate shipping & handling charges and any applicable sales tax (see charts above).

Card # _____ Exp. Date _____

Signature _____

Name _____Title _____

Company _____

Street Address _____

City _____ State _____ Zip _____

Business Phone (_____) _____ Fax (_____) _____

E-mail_____

BUSINESS REPLY MAIL

FIRST CLASS MAIL   PERMIT NO 68   CINCINNATI, OH

POSTAGE WILL BE PAID BY ADDRESSEE

The National Underwriter Co.
Orders Department #2-BB
P.O. Box 14448
Cincinnati, OH 45250-9786

NO POSTAGE
NECESSARY
IF MAILED
IN THE
UNITED STATES

BUSINESS REPLY MAIL

FIRST CLASS MAIL   PERMIT NO 68   CINCINNATI, OH

POSTAGE WILL BE PAID BY ADDRESSEE

The National Underwriter Co.
Orders Department #2-BB
P.O. Box 14448
Cincinnati, OH 45250-9786

POWER
NETWEAVING

10 Secrets to Successful Relationship Marketing

ROBERT S. LITTELL
CLU, ChFC, FLMI, SRM

DONNA FISHER

The
NATIONAL
UNDERWRITER
Company
PROFESSIONAL PUBLISHING GROUP

PO Box 14367
Cincinnati, OH 45250-0367
1-800-543-0874
www.nationalunderwriter.com

Cover and layout design: Jason T. Williams

ISBN: 0-87218-299-1

Library of Congress Control Number: 2001091390

Copyright © 2001
The National Underwriter Company
P.O. Box 14367, Cincinnati, Ohio 45250-0367

Printed in U.S.A.

ACKNOWLEDGMENTS

As those who read this book will learn, NetWeaving, an altruistic and outwardly focused gratuitous form of networking, is a concept as well as a philosophy. For many, NetWeaving is a way of life. Part of the joy of writing this book was to gather real life stories from successful professionals within the financial services industry who have been NetWeaving for most of or over their entire careers.

A book that simply explained this new term—NetWeaving™— as well as the strategies and habits that individuals can build into their daily practices would not have done justice to the altruism that is often the real basis for their NetWeaving acts. As you will see, simple acts of kindness, graciousness, friendship and sharing often are the sole inspiration for NetWeaving's beginnings. You will also see that, time and time again, just as a single stone is thrown into a still pond and the ever-expanding, concentric circles move far beyond the initial point of impact, so it is with NetWeaving.

You will also recognize that although altruism, at some level, may have been the motivation behind the NetWeaver's actions, the benefits that eventually inured back to the NetWeaver were often far beyond what the NetWeaver might have dreamed possible. We truly believe—Good things happen to people who *make* good things happen.

We owe a debt of gratitude to those listed below who agreed to share their stories, and to their friends, clients, prospects and others who were the beneficiaries of their NetWeaving activities.

If any one thing would help build credibility, trust and respect for the financial services industry, NetWeaving would be close to the top of that list. The contributions that these NetWeavers are making in their local communities, to society and to the viability of our overall economy are evidenced not only by the stories included in this book, but far beyond. Show us any inveterate NetWeaver and we'll show you someone who is making a difference in other people's lives on a daily basis.

Contributors in alphabetical order:

Jack Baker, CLU, AEP
Beverly Brooks, CLU, AEP
B.B. Brown, CLU, ChFC
Wally Dale, CLU, CPCU
Doug Duncan, J.D., LL.M.
Hank George
Terri Getman, J.D., CLU, ChFC
Art Gifford, CPA
Tony Gordon
Bill Grubb, CLU
Doug Hesse, CFP
Clark Howard
Harry V. Lamon, Esq.
Jeff McCart, CPCU
Clark McCleary, CLU, ChFC, MSFS
Rich Magner, CLU
Bill O'Quin, CLU, ChFC
Rodney Owens, J.D.
Russ Prince
Tom Rogerson
Steve Roy, J.D.
Hervey Ross
Mark D. Schooler, CLU
John J. (Jeff) Scroggin, J.D., LL.M.
Houston Smith, CPA/PFS, AEP
Mike Thiessen, J.D.
Troy Taylor
Gary Williams
LaDale Young
Stanley Zimmerman

We would also like to acknowledge the work of Professor Kristen Renwick Monroe, Associate Professor of Politics and Associate Director of the Program in Political Psychology at the University of California, Irvine. Her book which we cite, *The Heart of Altruism*, explores the nature of altruism and helped us see that NetWeaving is a blend of altruism and made us recognize that the motivation of the NetWeaver was really insignificant in comparison to the end results.

TABLE OF CONTENTS

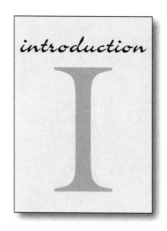

introduction

POWER
NETWEAVING™
STRATEGIC MATCHMAKING
FOR WIN-WIN RESULTS

"From what we get, we can make a living; what we give, however, makes a life."

– ARTHUR ASHE

Introduction

Well over a year ago, while we were sitting poolside in a lounge chair, my wife, Carolyn, suggested that I read a book she had just finished and thoroughly enjoyed. I asked her what the book was about and she said, "It's a great book about networking," and stressed that it had some great, practical tips on how to network better.

I must admit that my initial reaction toward reading a book on what I thought would be the typical "good ole boy" brand of networking—"You scratch my back and I'll scratch your's"—was not very appealing to me. I'd seen too many books that merely taught how to *use* (or abuse) your contact circle of friends, business associates, and centers of influence as a means of exchange—as a "gate of entry."

For several years I have been working on a concept that I refer to as "Do-a-Favr Marketing™" (DAFM); marketing according to the "Golden Rule." Do-a-Favr Marketing is built on the idea of doing favors for people, doing those favors over a long period of time, and asking nothing in return. It is also having the confidence to know that, sooner or later, those favors will pay off, sometimes in a very big way.

One of the most important elements of DAFM is a term that I dubbed "NetWeaving." The concept behind the word is how to build your business by becoming a first-class, strategic matchmaker between and among your clients and prospects, as well as learning how to become an invaluable strategic resource or resource provider.

Nevertheless, I figured there had to be at least a couple of good ideas in the book my wife recommended that somehow might fit within the context of my vision of a "kinder and gentler" form of networking. So I picked up the book and read on. To my amazement, I found myself nodding at points on almost every page. I was underlining and highlighting so many passages that I knew I had to buy Carolyn another copy of the book. Written by Donna Fisher and Sandy Vilas, *Power Networking* is all about win/win networking and relationship marketing.

Donna's book incorporated many of the principles that I had included as part of my NetWeaving strategy. I telephoned her out of the blue—both to compliment her and Sandy on their great book as well as to convey to her my thoughts about Do-a-Favr Marketing. I also wanted to discuss the "NetWeaving" term I had coined and the book of the same name that I had begun to write.

We had a great conversation and during our visit, Donna admitted that she had been searching for a term that better communicated the model of win/win networking that she described in her book. It encouraged me that she truly liked the warmer and non-self-serving sound of the term "NetWeaving." It then seemed perfectly natural for us to decide to author a book together, one that would focus on systems and strategies for connecting people in order to create those win/win relationships while also becoming a more proficient resource provider. Taking the word "Power" from Donna's title and the "NetWeaving" term from Do-a-Favr Marketing, we decided upon the logical title for this new book—Power NetWeaving.

If you're looking for a system that will make you rich overnight, this isn't the book for you. Although you might luck out and connect the *right* people in a win/win relationship that turned into an instant success, it is not that typical. Most often, like a good wine, NetWeaving takes time for the created relationship to age and mellow; for trust in the information and resources you provide to be established, and for the end product to percolate. Yet, months, or sometimes even years, down the road after the strategic matchmaking has paid big dividends, or when your resource information has saved a great deal of money or made someone a great deal of money, you will become a hero. In addition, you will become the logical choice to handle whatever specific products or services are needed: insurance or insurance advice, financial, estate or retirement planning, investment or tax guidance, assistance with asset management, trust services and much, much more.

When the benefits come, they will be plentiful and they won't just be in the form of using your products or services. You might receive other benefits such as:

- business being referred back to you;

- requests seeking your counsel for other projects or situations;

- referrals to influential people because they *like* the way you do business and your "give, *not* take" style;

- a sense of fulfillment that you are doing something that actually makes a difference in other people's lives.

Over a number of years, your NetWeaving pipeline will fill up and your prospecting days will be over. Your reputation as a match-maker and resource provider will make you an "in-demand" person.

If you are already a "NetWeaver," this book will help you become a *power* NetWeaver. If you like the concept of building your business by helping people build theirs, but have been lacking a strategic system to help you achieve more matchmaking and resource providing opportunities, then this book will show you how to systematically network while keeping your personal integrity, as well as the personal touch, intact.

In addition, this book will showcase a number of real life examples of how some of the most talented people in the financial services industry have built their reputations and businesses by being a NetWeaver, often subconsciously, and without any real strategy or plan for doing it consistently as a mode of operation.

As you learn more about NetWeaving and become more of a Power NetWeaver, names of clients and prospects and situations will pop into your head reminding you of the times when you were a NetWeaver, or when you could have been one, but didn't think about it.

Over time, your NetWeaving will craft a NetWeaver's quilt—a tapestry of valuable and influential contacts you've sewn together who have all grown to know you as a strategic matchmaker as well as a strategic resource; someone who cares more about helping other people instead of just benefiting himself. Someday, when you look back over your career, your NetWeaving experiences will stand out as some of your brightest and most satisfying moments. You'll be able to recall them with a great sense of pride, much like the successful teachers or coaches who are able to look back and see grown-up success stories—responsible leaders and winners whose lives they touched many years before. Or, as Mary Smith, secretary in the accounting firm of Smith & Raab (and wife of one of my favorite CPAs, Houston Smith) put it, "NetWeaving helps other people pull together the threads of their lives."

Join Donna and me on our special journey. You'll enjoy the trip.

Bob Littell
Donna Fisher

chapter

1

NETWEAVERS - THEY'RE EVERYWHERE
(YOU MIGHT BE ONE AND NOT KNOW IT.)

"It is one of the most beautiful compensations of this life that no man can sincerely try to help another without helping himself."

— RALPH WALDO EMERSON

Clark McCleary, CLU, ChFC, MSFS, longtime Guardian agent and past president of the Society of Financial Service Professionals, together with a friend, acted as both strategic coach and cheerleader for his neighbor, a casualty of corporate downsizing. Clark later helped, as strategic matchmaker, to put his neighbor together with another friend who then formed a new company. At the outset, they had no idea what would eventually become of the situation. And neither Clark nor his friend had the word "NetWeaving™" to describe what they had done.

Like so many others, Clark's NetWeaving story started out simply as a good deed that he was doing for a friend in need. It turned into something whose favorable consequences could never have been foreseen up front. After the two parties came together to form the business, Clark and his friend brought in all the experts to work as a team to put the new organization together—the attorney, the accountant and the business and liability insurance risk managers.

Twelve years later, that thriving business sold out to a publicly traded company.

Not only did Clark write all the insurance for the corporation's various needs all along the way, including substantial estate planning coverage and a ten-person salary continuation plan, but the two individuals ended up forming a new enterprise after they had fulfilled their non-compete requirements as stipulated in the clause in the contract. Guess who also wrote all of the coverage on the new business?

How many times have you heard people describe something they've done, of which they are very proud, and say to yourself, "I've done that, too!" That's why, as you read this book, you'll probably notice that you have applied some NetWeaving principles in your daily life. Almost everyone has done *some* NetWeaving; it's just that we *all* should be doing more.

Well over a decade ago, Bob Littell learned about the power of NetWeaving first-hand, and more by accident than intention. In that instance, Bob was invited to be a part of the teaching faculty for a seminar on estate planning that was being put together by a company that produces seminars around the country on various technical insurance and planning topics. While the company doesn't pay anything for the teaching aspect, they tell you the exposure you receive should be payment enough, and that certainly was the case for Bob. For this particular seminar, Bob was asked to be the expert life insurance agent on the program that also included an attorney and CPA.

Not very long after the seminar, Bob received a call from an attorney who had attended the seminar as a participant; he asked if Bob would join him for lunch. The attorney indicated that he would soon be leaving private practice to help run his family's out-of-state business. He asked Bob if he could buy some of his time in order to gain some advice regarding insurance and related planning issues. Bob insisted on not charging the attorney for the advice, shared information on a number of topics the attorney needed to keep in mind and answered a variety of other questions. Bob didn't think anything more about it; he simply considered his actions good public relations.

Without realizing what he was doing, Bob was NetWeaving—acting as a gratuitous information resource provider.

Shortly after the seminar, Bob ran into the attorney who had also appeared on the same program. At his request, Bob provided some NetWeaving (i.e. resource information) at no charge for one of the attorney's clients who was receiving some very questionable advice from another planner. As a result of Bob's guidance, not only did the client avoid some major problems, but Bob and the attorney became best of friends and even collaborated on a project that later attained national attention. As Bob found out, the benefits of NetWeaving are often large and often totally unforeseen and unexpected.

A couple of years passed and one day Bob's attorney friend, Jeff Scroggin, J.D., LL.M., called and indicated that he had been retained by a particular family (likewise as a result of the introduction from the seminar) to do the family's estate and business planning.

Specifically, they requested that Bob come in and provide some recommendations concerning their life insurance needs. The entire family has since become one of Bob's largest clients, as well as good friends, and he has become their trusted insurance advisor.

It's also interesting to note that Bob's estate planning attorney friend, Jeff, is also one of the best NetWeavers Bob has ever known. In Bob's words, "Jeff is constantly doing favors for his clients and looking for ways to network them with others where there might be mutual benefits. I know of at least one situation where he helped put a client in business and then later helped find a buyer for that business, and he wasn't looking to make anything personally on the sale."

A number of the most successful people in the financial services business have attracted their largest clientele or have been "referred in" as a direct or indirect result of their NetWeaving activities. Most of the professionals just didn't recognize that's what they were doing; even if they did, they would typically not be prepared to do it consistently.

NetWeaving is all about putting other people together in win/win relationships that will solve problems, satisfy needs or result in new or expanded business opportunities. It's also all about making yourself available as part of a resource network. This gratuitous strategic matchmaking and resource providing improves the situation or quality of others' lives.

It's a refreshing way of bringing the Golden Rule back into the mainstream of our lives and our world, especially in a business context. In her book, *Power Networking*, Donna Fisher makes a reference to the *Golden Rule of Networking*: "Give unto others as you would have them give unto you." That rule amplifies the importance of being considerate, giving, sharing and being respectful of self and others and, most importantly, putting others' interests first. That is the basis for NetWeaving.

NetWeaving works because it is people connecting with and enriching other people—for good. It's diametrically opposed to the back-slapping, good ole boy "take and use" form of networking which is internally focused on how *I* alone can benefit from *my* network of contacts and centers of influence.

NetWeaving is externally focused. It's all about giving and helping *others* while having the confidence to know that eventually you, the NetWeaver, will benefit in return.

Show us almost any top successful person in any industry, excluding the flash in the pan overnight success who cuts corners to get there, and we'll show you someone who is incorporating at least some of the elements of *Power NetWeaving* into his daily life and business practices.

Without even thinking, when one of the NetWeaver's clients or friends mentions that he has a problem, a desire for something or a great idea, but doesn't know where to go with it, the natural NetWeaver plants and records that fact in his subconscious. He then begins searching his mental Rolodex for someone or something that might be the answer to the question, dilemma or opportunity.

In those situations where the NetWeaver has a missing Rolodex card—a missing square in his NetWeaver's Resource and Information quilt—the best NetWeavers send out a mental "Help Wanted" signal to their subconscious. That is done so the NetWeaver can be on the lookout for a person who can supply the necessary information, a needed product or service or that someone who can help the client implement a great idea that has just been sitting there. When the resource is located, the "Help Wanted" sign comes down for that assignment.

When the NetWeaver comes across another situation where a prospect or client is in need of help with any of the NetWeaving categories, the NetWeaver's brain reacts. The circumstances go into the mental Rolodex and the brain retrieves the name(s) of the possible resource(s). The NetWeaver then focuses on becoming a strategic matchmaker.

The NetWeaving Diagram

Think of NetWeaving this way. At any point in time, every one of us has his or her own unique set of Needs, Problems, Ideas, and Opportunities, as well as the need for some kind of Information. And for each one of those, somewhere out there is a corresponding set of products, services, solutions and information resources that will ideally fill those needs. The goal is to find a solution to a problem, provide information or answers, or help in locating just that right person who can take a great idea and actually help make it a reality.

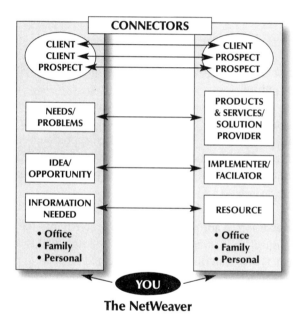

The NetWeaver

Many old-time financial services professionals reading this book will remember the TV show *Sergeant Bilko* played by Phil Silvers. Whether it was a lowly private or a four-star general, everyone knew that if you needed something, no matter what it was, Sergeant Bilko would get it for you. He was the ultimate strategic matchmaker and resource provider. Even today you may hear a reference made about someone who is renowned as a resource provider or strategic connector as being "a regular Sgt. Bilko."

In later chapters, we'll cover each of these connector categories in detail.

Needs and Problems May Be Recognized or Unrecognized

In some cases, we are fully aware of a need or problem we might have. In other situations, we may not be consciously aware of it but when it's exposed and brought to our attention, that small act alone might prove very valuable and enlightening.

Take the example of a client of yours who has an employee who just isn't cutting it, or who is so abrasive that he or she is doing the company more harm than good. Having the courage to bring that to the attention of your client is risky but it just might be the trigger that is needed to take action. The client will often appreciate your candor and, since many of us tend to procrastinate over making difficult people decisions, might have known about the problem all along but fail to acknowledge and act upon it.

In addition to adroitly bringing the problem into the open, an accomplished NetWeaver might even go one step further and compassionately help find the solution. That could range from providing the name of a resource who could offer sensitivity training to the employee to suggesting the name of, or even making an introduction to, a possible replacement candidate.

Business, Family, and Personal Needs and Problems

Some of these connector concepts fall within the realm of being business related such as a need for technology help, solving cash flow or financing problems, establishing a current valuation of the company's worth or finding a part-time CFO for a company that is not large enough to afford a full-time position. Some will relate to home and family (e.g., the name of a reliable builder when you learn the client is renovating a home), while others are of a more private nature relating to the person with whom you're communicating. Examples here include a need to improve public speaking skills, the desire to begin a health and fitness program, the request for a personal coach, the desire to reduce stress, etc.

This book will start by examining the altruistic nature behind NetWeaving as well as the psychology. It will then progress to show you how to create and implement, or just enhance, NetWeaving strategies that will not only help your prospects and clients, but will build your NetWeaving business beyond your wildest expectations. Finally, becoming a successful and consistent NetWeaver will increase your personal satisfaction with your career and with the role you play in improving other people's lives.

A Contradiction Between NetWeaving Principles and Strategies?

One might ask if there isn't a contradiction between the warmth and genuineness of the *principles* behind the NetWeaving philosophy and the *strategies* that planners and other financial services professionals must *implement* in order to become an accomplished NetWeaver.

Just as in a religious, political, or philosophical context, the purity of the principles and beliefs are inextricably connected with the strategies involved with getting the word out amongst the multitude. *Both* are essential. The most principled, idealistic, well-intentioned politician will never have a chance to implement her philosophies and beliefs until and unless she is elected to office. That involves establishing and implementing successful strategies.

Therefore, we say this book is about teaching people how to strategically NetWeave. For those who are already applying many

NetWeaving techniques, this book will improve your radar and make you more aware of NetWeaving opportunities. However, simply improving your existing skills is not enough. To become a *power* NetWeaver, one must build the practice of NetWeaving into his or her daily life.

NetWeaving goes far beyond traditional customer service and we already know that providing customers with exceptional service leads to exceptional results. When people are served and treated well they come back for more. The same principles apply in all areas of life. When we are served and treated well, we return again and again.

What comes to most people's mind when they think of Nordstrom or the Ritz Carlton? The words "quality" and "service" come up over and over again. Why is that? It's because Nordstrom and the Ritz Carlton have focused on developing a reputation for quality and service—above expectations. They go the extra mile. Their employees treat a customer as someone special. Those businesses have trained their personnel in the people skills that generate warmth, connection, caring and service. They also empower their employees to solve problems themselves in order to make the customer happy.

NetWeaving elevates customer service to an entirely new level. It is the NetWeaver who takes the initiative and empowers himself to act upon those unexpected things that are in the NetWeaver's toolkit— matchmaking and resource providing.

A simple example of NetWeaving (the resource provider aspect) that we see occasionally in the world of retail might involve a Nordstrom's sales clerk who, when asked for something the store doesn't carry, refers the customer to another store, possibly one of its biggest competitors. Now that's good service, but not really that much out of the ordinary.

What would you think if the sales clerk not only told you the name of the other store but picked up the phone to call the competitor to determine if it had it in stock, and in your size, the item you wanted? That would be an example of outrageous NetWeaving; being a real, live resource for others. In any case, that unselfish gesture would make a lasting impression on you. Rather than losing business, the gratuitous, outrageous and unexpected service you received would work to attract more business in the long run.

Here's a real life story from the financial services industry of how being the source of a referral can be just as good as, if not better than, being the resource yourself.

Terri Getman, J.D., CLU, ChFC, an advanced underwriting attorney for PruSelect in Minneapolis, Minnesota, has been doing a fair amount of "SERP Swapping" in the last year or so. For those not familiar with the term, SERP stands for Supplemental Executive Retirement Plan, also known more generically as non-qualified deferred compensation. It's a plan that many companies use to reward certain key individuals and executives. Because of the way it's designed and to whom it's offered, the plan allows the company to pick and choose among key employees rather than cover all the employees as in a normal retirement plan. It's also common where highly compensated executives are actually penalized by the company retirement plan. That is especially true of a 401(k) plan where, as a percentage of income, they are being discriminated against in relation to how much of their pre-retirement income they'll be able to supply for their post-retirement years.

With the growth of the stock market, as well as employer stock options and other successful investments, fortunes have been amassed by many of these key people. Rather than needing more income, these individuals actually require more life insurance for estate liquidity and other purposes. That's where the "swap" comes in; split dollar life insurance gets exchanged for the SERP plan.

In a particular case, Terri was brought in as the expert and thought she was going to be simply explaining the who, how and when of SERP swaps. What happened was that the real issues the client had concerned accounting for employee stock options. Although Terri could have given a few broad answers, she felt obligated to provide the client with what she would have wanted had she been in the client's situation—the best possible expert information. Through her industry NetWeaving contacts, Terri knew that the most knowledgeable person in the area was Mark Titlebaum, with Phoenix-Home, a competitor. Nevertheless, Terri referred the question to Mark who ended up handling the case.

The trust that Terri earned by making a selfless recommendation to do what was in the client's best interests earned her the reputation of being a true NetWeaving resource. Her share of the business has been repaid to her many times more than what she gave away to others.

NETWEAVING EXERCISE #1

How to Recognize a NetWeaver

Have you already acted as a NetWeaver? Think of a past situation that involved a client of yours (or even a potential customer) who had a need for a product or service or the solution to a problem where *you* served as the connector—the one who put the parties together. (Refer to the diagram found on page 7.)

1. Have you ever strategically matched up a client or prospect with a resource person to fulfill a need or solve a problem? Have you helped to enrich, facilitate or implement ideas or opportunities that someone else had? What was the outcome?

2. Have you ever been a resource provider for someone, either acting in that capacity yourself or where you referred the person in need to someone in your network of providers of resource information?

3. Have you ever been a NetWeaver between one of your clients and a prospect with whom you've never done business before? What was the outcome?

4. Have you ever matched up two non-client prospects with whom you've been working, putting them together in a win/win relationship? What was the outcome?

5. How did you first come up with the idea to NetWeave in each of these circumstances?

6. Do you consistently look for other opportunities like those mentioned? If not, why?

chapter

2

THE NETWEAVER'S MINDSET
(THE PHILOSOPHY)

"A person starts to live when he can live outside himself."

— ALBERT EINSTEIN

A philosophy engulfs the heart and soul. It controls and conducts the symphony of our emotions. Just as the symphony conductor must learn all the nuances of all the instruments in the orchestra to be most effective, the same is true for the power NetWeaver. He must learn a variety of NetWeaving™ strategies and skills and then surround himself with the broadest possible array of NetWeaving resource contacts. Those NetWeavers are non-traditional thinkers who are attracted by the harmony of the NetWeaving philosophy and they will be enriched as they learn to hone their skills. Their audiences are also their clients, prospects and friends, and it is they who will become the ultimate beneficiaries of the NetWeaver's overall genius and mastery. Learn to become a NetWeaving maestro.

The Philosophy of NetWeaving

NetWeaving is built upon the Golden Rule: "Do unto others as you would have them do unto you." It's an altruistic and gratuitous form of networking.

If your assignment on earth was to help others and you didn't have to worry about making a living, on which of these two functions would you probably spend most of your time?

1. Since no man is an island and very few things can be accomplished by one person without the help or assistance of others, one primary role would be to constantly be on the lookout for opportunities to put people together in situations that would benefit them both.

2. The problem for many of us is not that we aren't getting *enough* information on a project or task; rather, it's information overload. We must find a way to sort through, prioritize, filter out and end up with just the right information or resources that will best fit what we're trying to accomplish. We need to encounter people who can provide

reliable, expert resources or locate those who are very well-connected—a sort of walking Yellow Pages.

When you really examine NetWeaving, it's just a new approach to relation-based marketing. Yet, it represents a whole new set of clubs in the bag and it requires a set of skills that, if and when perfected, make the resource NetWeaver irreplaceable.

A Word of Caution

The philosophy of NetWeaving promotes qualities and evokes adjectives like altruistic, unselfish, caring, sharing, symbiotic and benevolent. Although agents and planners should become aware and begin practicing some elements of NetWeaving from their first days in their practice or profession, NetWeaving is a concept that individuals who are brand new to the financial services industry should wade into rather than take an instant plunge.

In fact, for insurance agents, financial planners, registered reps and others who are new to the industry and dependent upon commission income, there can be as much danger in it as there are benefits since the rewards of NetWeaving are often long-term in nature. The good feelings that are generated and the sense of satisfaction from having helped someone by strategic matchmaking or resource providing only goes so far when your income is totally based on commissions or transaction-oriented fees. Likewise, since most new individual's NetWeaving activities won't typically have sufficient time to blossom into something big enough to create unexpected but often generous returned benefits to the NetWeaver, warm regards and good relationships generated by NetWeaving will usually only go so far as a substitute for new account business and revenue.

It's not that helping put clients and prospects together in win/win relationships, even for people brand new to any of the financial services professions, isn't great for their business in the long run. Rather, it's that NetWeaving can often be time-consuming and seemingly a non-productive use of time that best fits those who are already well-established in the business.

One element of NetWeaving that even neophytes to the financial services industry should begin practicing on a daily basis is to expand their resource contacts and their knowledge base of useful information. They should learn how to nurture their resource contacts. During the beginning stages of their careers, they should be in the information and resource *gathering* mode.

Those who survive the trial period, usually the first three to five years, should be ready to expand their NetWeaving skills. For the more senior financial services professionals who have reached the point of success and income in their lives and careers, where they are looking for more than just additional sales or higher fee and investment income, NetWeaving offers them the greatest of all opportunities.

In terms of Abraham Maslow's hierarchy of needs, these individuals have reached the stage of self-actualization where they have passed through their stage of personal ego and needs gratification. Instead, they are looking for something more enriching and satisfying. It's not that income and assets are no longer important, it's just that these people are looking for more out of life.

NetWeaving is what many 40+-year olds in the financial services industry who have burned out or plateaued are yearning for; something to re-energize their careers and instill a purpose and a worthwhile mission to what they are doing. They are looking for something that can help answer some of the questions which many people in the financial services industry are searching for today.

- How can I make a bigger difference in other people's lives?

- How can I leave some kind of lasting imprint? How has my walking around on this planet, for the brief period each one of us has, actually made some difference in a number of people's lives?

- How can I give back and share some of the fruits of my bounty?

- How can I become more externally focused?

- How can I become a mentor for others? How can I explain some of the true secrets to happiness in life? How can I awaken them to the mystery of genuine fulfillment earlier than I experienced it?

Changing from WIIFM to WIIFY

In a philosophical sense, people might not recognize they are engaged in NetWeaving. Briefly explain the concept of NetWeaving to someone, though, and notice how frequently a smile crosses his face as he is reminded of something he has done along those lines. Maybe it triggers the thought of a friend or contact he knows who handles his business that way. Benevolent, externally focused, strategic matchmaking, as well as providing information and resources to and for others, is just so logical and it makes so much common sense. It's unfortunate that more people don't do it, or don't do it more often.

NetWeaving isn't available as a college course; it must be learned in the real world. Maybe it's better that way since a certain level of maturity must be reached before NetWeaving becomes acceptable behavior. After you truly embrace the concept in your everyday life and activities, tell people why NetWeaving has become an important part of your life and watch how people immediately light up to you.

Yet having a philosophy of NetWeaving is not enough. To paraphrase a popular saying, "Ideas are a dime a dozen, but the person who can make an idea become a reality is priceless." Concepts, ideas and philosophies are just words on paper until someone puts them to work with strategies and, eventually, a concrete action plan. When you stop thinking "WIIFM" (What's In It For Me) and start thinking

"WIIFY" (What's In It For You), you will be ready to begin learning how to become a strategic NetWeaver.

NetWeaving Sometimes Covers a Lifetime

One of Bob's good friends has carved out a national reputation, not only as one of the top qualified retirement plan attorneys in the country (he drafted the first prototype Keogh/HR-10 plan and handled one of the first professional corporation cases decided by the United States Supreme Court that allowed professionals for the first time to incorporate their practices and utilize qualified retirement plans), but also as a NetWeaver in both senses of the term. He is both a strategic matchmaker and a strategic resource provider.

Harry V. Lamon, Esq., related a story that accentuates another difference between networking and NetWeaving. For many, when they think of networking, they recall a single event that flows in one direction.

Harry emphasized that NetWeaving is a *way of life*. It often involves a string of events that are connected, although not always visible at the time, and which end up being woven into the NetWeaver's tapestry over time.

Harry's first childhood playmate is still one of his best friends to this day. From playing together in the schoolyard, to becoming Eagle Scouts together in the same troop, to college fraternity brothers at Davidson University, to being in each other's wedding, Harry and his friend have not only remained close but they have inspired and challenged each other to become better at every turn in life.

One of Harry's greatest passions is the Salvation Army. His involvement began in 1962 when he joined the Atlanta board and served as the national chair from 1991 until 1993. Harry was able to persuade his friend to become involved and today they both share the passion.

Not only did Harry's NetWeaving provide the Salvation Army with an outstanding new resource, as a result of his friend's dedicated service, but Harry's publicity-shy, unassuming friend was presented with Atlanta's annual community service honor, the Shining Light Award. At the same time, it provided Harry's friend with some of the most personally satisfying and rewarding experiences of his lifetime.

Now it's time to focus on strategies for NetWeaving.

NetWeaving Philosophy Testimonials

Rodney Owens, J.D., a high profile estate planning attorney in Dallas, Texas, with the firm of Meadows, Owens, and Collier, quoted a well-known client of his who, when Rodney was very new to the planning world, very matter-of-factly made a comment that has stuck with him all these years:

No one, without exception, can attain any degree of success without at least one other person wanting and permitting it to occur.

Rodney went on to very eloquently describe his idea of NetWeaving:

This could be that first introduction; that first speaking or writing opportunity; that initial business contact. Any truly successful person, looking back, can trace an identifiable event, sometimes long forgotten, that pushed him or her to a new level allowing them to start the journey towards success. And we carry this element within us as we progress, many times oblivious to the web of influence that we are weaving along the way. In the day-to-day confluence of our lives, we simply have no idea or realization of the sphere of influence over which we create contacts, nor the rippling effects of our actions in "connecting" people. We simply make it happen as a form of a sixth sense, a natural way, so to speak, of conducting ourselves on personal and business matters. And the more relationships we automatically share, the wider our network of business resources become.

Gary Williams, a consistent Million Dollar Round Table (MDRT) Top of the Table insurance professional in Atlanta, Georgia, has made NetWeaving an integral part of his daily routine.

Helping clients find products or services or just information for which they have a need, totally outside the insurance realm, separates me from other agents who are simply trying to sell something. I've also found that by working closely with attorneys and CPAs, identifying work that clients of theirs are delaying or avoiding, and then becoming a catalyst to help get that work done—referring it back to the attorney or CPA—earns me a constant flow of referrals. I'm frankly amazed at how few agents do this.

I find that if I take care of my clients, listen carefully and then help them match their needs with others in my resource network who have solutions, I become one of their most valuable resources.

Art Gifford, senior partner in the CPA firm of Gifford, Hillegass, and Ingwersen, has been NetWeaving as long as he can remember. A high profile CPA in Dunwoody, Georgia, just outside Atlanta, Art started out simply NetWeaving but has now grown it into a new business.

Early in Dr. Tom Stanley's career, author of several best selling books including *The Millionaire Next Door*, Art not only appeared in Tom's book but was cited as one of the best examples of how a CPA can perform in the role of strategic resource provider. What started out as NetWeaving has now grown into a profitable part of Art's business.

Art's "networking strategy" simply focuses on providing value to clients and network service providers. When positive contributions are made to the various parts of the networking process, recipients generally respond by returning gracious returns to the NetWeaver. These returns can come in the form of happy paying clients, referrals, and more work or sales. Usually the more you give in life will directly reflect in what you receive in return.

NETWEAVING
EXERCISE #2

1. Based upon what you've read so far about NetWeaving, write down your personal NetWeaving Mission Statement.

2. Write out how you will go about surrounding yourself with contacts, resources and information that will enable you to become a better resource yourself.

3. Begin thinking of this as a daily affirmation: "I am an expert NetWeaver. I consistently look for opportunities to be a strategic matchmaker, to help put people together in win/win relationships. I am also constantly on the lookout for ways to become a better strategic resource of contacts, information and ideas."

The NetWeaver's Creed

•   I will consistently be on the lookout for opportunities to put people together in win/win relationships without concern for what I will get out of it.

•   I will shift from thinking about WIIFM (What's In It For Me) to WIIFY (What's In It For You).

•   I will learn to be a resource for others, both regarding the types of information I can provide as well as to surround myself with resource contacts who can be of service to those with whom I come in contact.

•   I will apply the principles of NetWeaving on a daily basis and will make a habit of doing those things that will allow me to best implement NetWeaving strategies.

chapter 3

THE PSYCHOLOGY
OF NETWEAVING

*"Complete possession is proved only by giving.
All you are unable to give possesses you."*

— ANDRE GIDE

Why do people do favors for others or go out of their way to help one another? Is it because of pure altruism, or is it really done in order to obtain something in return? Pure altruism generally means doing something for someone else without any thought for the consequences (good or bad) that might benefit or befall the person doing something for another.

To explain this concept, psychologists at one end of the spectrum (who from a psychological perspective are more determined in their approach and beliefs) might try to explain altruism as a series of genetically inherited traits that have evolved in the human race. An example in the animal world might be seen in a situation where a mother bird or a deer distracts a predator or sacrifices its own life to save her offspring. Those embracing a genetic or evolutionary theory might even go further saying that form of biological altruism was imprinted to preserve the species. In human evolutionary terms, if everyone always acted out of self-interest, civilization, as we know it, might not have been possible and many of the most amazing achievements of mankind might never have been accomplished.

At the other extreme, behavioral psychologists would more likely consider altruism as a learned behavior, a sort of stimulus response activity where the mouse is rewarded for performing a certain action and learns to repeat that action over and over again. We grow up learning sayings such as:

- "One good turn deserves another,"

- "Do unto others as you would have them do unto you," and

- "'Tis better to give than to receive."

We not only learn that when we are altruistic it helps others, but we find out that it often results in personal recognition for what we've done. On top of that, if we honestly admit it, altruism also makes us feel good and, in a way, both of those are actually forms of pleasurable self-interest.

We ascribe more to a theory proposed by Professor Kristen Renwick Monroe, Associate Professor of Politics and Associate Director of the Program in Political Psychology at the University of California, Irvine. In her book *The Heart of Altruism*[1], Monroe views altruism more as a "continuum" where at one end, the altruistic behavior is just motivated by pure egoistic self-interest while at the other end of the continuum it's done out of the purest of unselfish motives; sheer acts of genuine benevolence and self-sacrifice. Much of what Professor Monroe writes about in her book concerns the pure forms of altruism; acts of bravery as were exhibited by those individuals who risked their own and sometimes their family's lives to hide Jews during the Nazi times in Germany and Austria; or the people who in an act of courage rush into a burning building to try and save a total stranger. When Professor Monroe asked them why they put their lives at risk, their response was often, "It just happened so suddenly—I just did it instinctively."

We think that altruism, as it relates to NetWeaving™, is a mixture of all these things. Sometimes we act out of what might be termed pure altruism—instinctive behavior (whether it is biological or genetic in nature is irrelevant) while at other times we do it purely for egoistic or selfish reasons. There are many shades in between.

For the purpose of this book, we are not going to be judgmental by trying to pinpoint the exact underlying motivation of the NetWeaver. We think that whether it is done out of almost pure altruism, sheer egoism or any gradient in between, other people will generally benefit and society will benefit from seeing more visual examples of altruism. The fact that the NetWeaver will often benefit in the long run should encourage others to do more of it.

Take the case of Beverly Brooks, CLU, AEP, past national president of the Society of Financial Service Professionals, and an insurance, estate planning and employee benefits specialist in Dallas, Texas.

In 1996, Beverly read a tragic story in the *Dallas Morning News* about a young teenage girl who had been hit by a truck on her walk to school and had been paralyzed. Libby's mother (a single mom) had to quit her job immediately after the accident in order to remain constantly by her daughter's bedside during her stay in the hospital. After Libby was allowed to go home, her fragile state of health required almost continuous attention by her mother, in addition to frequent visits and assistance by professional nurses. Libby also had a seven-year old brother who also required his mother's attention. Mounting medical bills and daily living expenses left the family in a financial crisis and they were literally 38 days away from being evicted from their home when Beverly went into action.

Beverly was so moved by the story that she decided she wasn't going to allow the eviction to happen. Through Beverly's efforts and the work of her universe of friends and their network of friends and contacts, over $50,000 was raised and a loan settlement negotiated. A trust was established to purchase the home for Libby's protection and the mortgage was paid in full.

As a direct result of some of the calls Beverly made to raise the money to save Libby's house, she also received calls from three individuals who needed life insurance and wanted to purchase it from her. What started out as a purely altruistic gesture and effort reaped new clients for Beverly. That's what makes NetWeaving so much fun. As is often the case, the more you give, the more you receive.

Another case of pure altruism involved one of Bob's favorite CPAs in Atlanta, Houston Smith, CPA/PFS, AEP, senior partner in the firm of Smith & Raab. Houston is one of a new breed of CPAs who have successfully made the transition from providing pure accounting service to providing much broader, total financial planning services. We suggest that it is largely due to his NetWeaving skills.

One of Houston's most memorable NetWeaving experiences exemplifies how NetWeaving doesn't always create a straight line benefit back to the NetWeaver, but instead provides psyche satisfaction and enhanced emotional energy from seeing the benefits of one's altruism in action. The financial rewards come indirectly as an offshoot of an enhanced reputation within his circle of peers where altruism, virtue and doing acts of kindness are revered. As we've said before, people want to do business with people who are making differences in other people's lives.

In this particular situation, a friend and fellow member of the Decatur, Georgia, Rotary Club told Houston a story about a tragedy in South Africa and a church's unique response to a cold-blooded act of mass murder.

About eight years ago, the news reported a massacre that took place within a small church in Cape Town, South Africa. Three black men burst into the church and opened fire with machine guns killing eight white people and wounding several others.

Rather than striking out to avenge the murders, the parishioners decided they should not only turn the other cheek, but also respond with an act of forgiveness and kindness. They decided to build a youth center within the run-down shanty community where the murderers probably lived which was adjacent to their white, middle class neighborhood. A local Cape Town chapter of the Rotarians helped raise the funds and the center was built. Unfortunately, they ran out of money and had nothing remaining to furnish the center.

That year Houston was in a position within the Rotary to have contacts not only at a local level but also at an international level. After helping his local Rotary Club raise $2,000, he was able to raise $8,000 more through matching challenges within the national and international arms of the Rotary. The total amount raised was equivalent to $25,000 Rand [South African currency unit] that was the exact amount needed to furnish the center.

In this case, you would probably call Houston's friend, who first brought the story to his attention, the initial NetWeaver. Houston, though, was in a unique position to put the right people together to accomplish the task so you might call this story NetWeaving squared.

As pointed out at the beginning, Houston gave no thought up front to how he would benefit personally from his involvement. As you can imagine, the entire story of how a tragedy was turned into a win/win situation for everyone involved created goodwill that warmed the entire organization. Since Houston does much of his business with Rotarians, there is no way of knowing just how much business was generated from his actions.

Here's another example of how NetWeaving not only made a believer out of an individual but made that individual richer both figuratively and literally.

Mark D. Schooler, CLU, principal, Schooler Insurance Services and founding and life member of the Top of the Table, has been fudging a little bit. Ever since we explained the concept of NetWeaving to him, he's been talking about NetWeaving because he, like others, had been looking for a term to describe what he spends at least a third of his total time doing. Mark has been living NetWeaving since early in his career when he decided that NetWeaving would be a way to differentiate himself from others in the insurance business. One well-known industry pro told Mark that many people within Mark's extensive centers of influence world have no clear idea of what he does for a living.

Mark describes his brand of NetWeaving as "Physically introducing people to each other" at a breakfast, lunch or dinner meeting or possibly over a glass or two of wine. In fact, one of his best NetWeaving stories came as a result of his assisting an executive in the wine industry in California find a similar position at an internationally known winery also in California. Partially as a result of interacting with the executive, the key California winery sponsored a series of wine tastings and dining in Dallas that has raised over $250,000 for a Dallas charity.

So far, you haven't seen any financial services stories but we can promise you that many will follow. When you're perceived as a NetWeaver, people *want* to do business with you and actually seek you out. People want to do business with people who make a difference in other people's lives and, ironically, many of the people who do that as a habit have been doing it even before their career reached the pinnacle of success they currently enjoy. In other words, they were NetWeaving before they attained their level of career success when they could have been financially concerned about the short-term impact of their decision. It's called conviction.

Mark's typical introduction is simple. When he first meets with the individual, whether it's a potential job opportunity, matching someone who has a need or problem with a product, service or solution provider, or putting someone with a need for money together with a money source, he says, "My purpose in getting the two of you together is for you to gain a better understanding of how each of you make money. After you both understand that, and determine if you have anything in common or if you can be of help to each other, the rest is up to you."

In another classic NetWeaving case study from eight or nine years ago, an influential banker referred Mark to one of his loan customers. Prior to that introduction, Mark had referred the bank officer to several of his clients who needed a new banking relationship. The bank's loan customer was so taken with Mark's matchmaking approach that he asked Mark to review his entire estate plan including wills and insurance policies. While the process itself took over five years to implement before the client finally agreed to put the plan into action (as is often the case with a workaholic client), over $30 million of permanent insurance was placed. The NetWeaving favor was returned many fold. Five years later and Mark is writing another $40 million of insurance, some for the estate and some for individual purposes.

Like Mark, many professionals within the entire financial services industry have discovered mutual NetWeaving—being in a position to introduce one professional to another as a resource individual and then making the introductions to potential clients—is one of the most productive areas of NetWeaving.

Through an introduction, made by an influential Dallas attorney, Mark came to know and became friends with a very bright young man, a protégé of the senior partner in a major New York investment and banking firm. The young man was being groomed to be a partner in a local venture with the New York investment banker. They were in the process of implementing some insurance planning with another insurance representative when the New York investment banker died. Over the years, that insurance representative had ignored the young dynamo and treated him like a kid in a man's world. All the while, Mark continued to NetWeave with the young man.

Guess who became the trusted advisor and insurance specialist for our young hard-charger when he assumed control of the firm? NetWeaving has been instrumental in everything from helping him become a wine connoisseur (i.e. being an information resource) to introducing him to a cutting edge estate planning attorney (i.e. matching a need with a product or service provider). The law firm now handles many of the legal issues for his company. The amount of insurance Mark has placed for estate and key person purposes is now approaching $50 million.

Nothing Is Wrong With Traditional Networking

Earlier we had contrasted NetWeaving with networking in a way that might sound derogatory toward networking; that is not the case. There is nothing inherently bad about networking. The fact that it may be focused on how to generate additional business for oneself does not mean it has negative connotations in and of itself unless the methods used to cultivate and harvest one's network of contacts are overly manipulative and exploitative. If someone learns NetWeaving and ends up mixing it up with "power brokering," meaning they are doing it with their own end in mind rather than what benefits the people they are matching up, they miss out on some of the deeply satisfying and long-term benefits of their good deeds.

Consultants get paid for NetWeaving in a power broker sense. It's usually part of their job description and it's certainly part of the reason why someone hires a consultant. Consultants often do NetWeaving as part of their ordinary course of business and their understood job function. However, if they're smart, they will always be looking for opportunities to mix in a good bit of quasi-altruistic matchmaking as well. Consultants are in a unique position to leverage their unusually broad and deep resource base of information and people.

Interweaving Traditional Networking With NetWeaving

When combining Networking and NetWeaving you will listen for opportunities to be a strategic matchmaker and be of service.

In a NetWeaving group, you're building your resource Rolodex—your personal Yellow Pages—and you're acting in the role of a NetWeaving Social Worker—"Who needs my help?" You are constantly asking yourself:

- "How can I help this person?"

- "Whom do I know with who I can match this person to solve his or her most pressing business problem?"

- "Whom do I know who has the greatest need for a particular product or service?"

- "How can I act as a resource for this person or do I know someone else who can become a valuable resource for this person?"

From a psychological perspective, it is actually much easier to carry on meaningful conversations since you will be talking about the other person rather than yourself.

Why not be the first in your city to form a NetWeaver's club and use the NetWeaver's Creed as your club's rules?

Bob, who has served on the board of the Buckhead Business Association (BBA) in Atlanta, has introduced the concept of NetWeaving to them. Early on he noticed two things:

1. The more people talk and think about NetWeaving, the more they are looking for opportunities to help others rather than just themselves.

2. The number of new members in the BBA has increased. Part of the reason might be attributable to the fact that as new potential members hear about NetWeaving and understand what it's all about, they decide they really want to be part of an organization dedicated to helping others.

A New Approach for a Client Review

In a conversation about NetWeaving with Mark Hendrix, an Ohio National agent and registered representative from Lexington, Kentucky, an idea popped out that could change the way we all do client reviews.

Imagine that at the end of a normal review, we added something along these lines:

"John, I really appreciate the trust you've placed in me as your (insurance agent, financial planner, CPA, attorney, investment advisor, etc.) and I'd like to be of even more value to you in the future than I've been in the past. I've embraced a new philosophy that is catching on in the financial services industry; it's called NetWeaving. It's a gratuitous form of networking that focuses on two things: first, putting *other* people together in win/win relationships and, secondly, acting as a strategic resource for others. By that I mean either serving in the resource providing capacity myself or offering my clients access to my network of resources who share the same NetWeaving philosophy.

"In order for me to be a better NetWeaver and strategic resource for you, I need to know some additional information about you and your business and what people or situations I should be on the look-out for which might be of help to you.

"It might be something as simple as putting you in touch with someone who shares the same hobbies and interests, or (add your own idea) or even helping match you up with someone who could be a source of new business for you. This strategic resource part extends to your personal and family situation as well as your business concerns. Therefore, if you're in the market for the name of a top flight real estate agent, home remodeler or technology expert (you pick the ones you have assembled) who could help your situation, from building a home network to setting up a home theater system, just let me know.

"My goal is to be a Sergeant Bilko or Corporal Klinger for you. Whether you were a general or a private, Sergeant Bilko or Corporal Klinger was the guy you went to when you needed something. Both of them had this incredible set of resources at their disposal and they prided themselves on being able to solve other people's problems. One of my goals is to become an indispensable resource for you, not only for what we've done in the past, but even more so for what we can do in the future."

[1] *The Heart of Altruism*, Kristen Renwick Monroe (Princeton University Press, Princeton, NJ 08540, 1996)

chapter

4

DEVELOPING POWER NETWEAVING STRATEGIES

"A good plan, violently executed now, is better than a perfect plan next week."

— GENERAL GEORGE S. PATTON

Spread the Word

Every person has contacts and information that can be of value to others. Imagine what it would be like if, in every conversation, people were listening to try and identify an opportunity to be a resource to someone else?

When I build a strong resource and information network, it benefits not just me but everyone in my contact network. When I assemble a vast, diverse and powerful network, I then have more information and contacts that I can share with others. When I grow my own network, I not only increase my own knowledge value, but I increase the value of what I have to offer others by virtue of my vast network. In addition, I can offer the growing wisdom that comes from learning from others.

Almost everyone you meet can become a resource for you and a connector for others. It's just that most people have not developed the strategic thinking muscle that will put the gears in place to make the connection. Just as importantly, it is a way to capture and categorize that information or resource for later retrieval.

But locked inside each one of us, that information or resource remains useless to ourselves and others. Like coal in the ground or a grain of sand in an oyster, both have great potential. But neither can the coal ever become a diamond nor the sand be the spark that becomes a pearl unless the right set of circumstances are present.

Become a strong proponent for the concept and value of NetWeaving™. Encourage others to be strategic matchmakers. Communicate to people that you want to be a resource for them and you'll create the environment for many diamonds and pearls.

NetWeaving Differs From Being a Power Broker

Some of history's most powerful people have been expert NetWeavers only in a very non-altruistic sense. In their times they were considered power brokers. Their influence and power were largely attributable to their network of contacts and resources and they leveraged those skills into great personal wealth. They recognized the value of being considered a resource—a gateway to persons of power. Much the same can be said of power brokers today, especially in the political arena. Being a power broker is one of the primary roles of a lobbyist. There's also a well-known, Middle Eastern arms dealer whose legendary power was so great he was able to deal with both sides involved in the same conflict. Neither side could afford to have him as an adversary.

As briefly mentioned in the previous chapter, the difference between being a power broker and a NetWeaver is that to a power broker, strategic matchmaking represents a means to an end rather than an end in and of itself. In other words, a power broker will say, "I'll open this door for you so you can access the right people, but I'll expect to receive something immediately in return for doing so." To a NetWeaver, the act of NetWeaving represents the end all by itself; nothing is expected up front in return. The end (i.e., additional sales, referrals, etc.) might or might not come, but the deed and the outcome are not connected nor contingent upon each other.

There is nothing wrong with power brokering. Many valuable, in-demand consultants serve in that role and it is a service that is considered by many to be of great worth. It is important to realize that you can easily get the two concepts mixed up and cause confusion and often hard feelings due to false expectations on either or both party's part.

Missed NetWeaving Opportunities

Too often, we take the obvious for granted and it often results in opportunities lost:

- We think people already know what we want and what they need. *Wrong.*

- We think people realize that we want to be a resource for them. *Wrong.*

- We think people have the same concept and understanding about networking as we have. *Wrong.*

As you can see, it is often our thinking that limits our opportunities. Never assume that others know what you want, or that you recognize what they need. By conditioning, even when they know you well, they will still assume that you are trying to sell them something. They aren't conditioned to NetWeaving and don't understand the philosophy and strategies behind it. Even if they did understand and saw you in that light doesn't mean they will remember it over time. That means they won't automatically picture you as a resource nor recall your value as a strategic matchmaker. You must keep reminding them. A personalized newsletter that highlights (without sounding boastful) some of your NetWeaving successes is a great way to keep your unique skill fresh in your client's and prospect's minds.

Why Is It Called Brainstorming?

Think of the brightest electrical storm you have ever seen; one bolt of lightning popping right after another, each one illuminating the sky and each one preceding a loud boom. Brainstorming, in the same way, will really start exploding when you develop strategic thinking as your norm. The boom following the illumination can make a great thundering roar, or a low-key thud. Some of your brainstorming ideas will result in a thundering success while others might be more like dull thuds. Success is a by-product for those who are willing to fail.

Most people never consistently set aside time to strategize or brainstorm. What if you always were in that creative mode? What if your mind was always cooking up ways to make something happen? Just like a comedian who is always seeing things through a specially focused lens that finds or creates humor in everyday circumstances and situations, the power NetWeaver is always seeing things through the lens of opportunity. It is a matter of constant brainstorming, looking for ways to connect, serve, do a favor, add a resource or create an opportunity.

Brainstorming and creativity are fostered by an environment of openness, non-judgmental thinking, trust and freedom. Rather than looking for exactly the right answer, it's more a matter of looking for another way, a new way, a better way or a different idea. In order to develop strategic thinking as the norm, those are the same qualities that must be fostered in your thinking environment—your mind. Rather than worrying about whether it is the perfect contact for which your prospect or client is searching, present one idea and that might lead to another idea…and so on…and the cycle continues.

Trust the Process

NetWeaving requires trust. You must trust the process just like you plant a seed and water it day after day with no sign of growth. You know that with the proper soil, water and sunlight the plant will grow. Once it pops out of the ground, the growth seems to accelerate. NetWeaving involves gathering and storing a great deal of information that won't be used until a later date, sometimes until much later. It also involves taking action and having the confidence to know that there will be favorable consequences even when there is no immediate, tangible evidence.

Most everything in life is a building process. Everything starts with an idea and then action and behaviors develop in support of that idea. A house requires a strong foundation or there will be major problems during the life of that house. A business requires a strong vision, business plan and consistent action in line with that business plan. A relationship requires nurturing and time for trust to be established. Actions must be seen by others as consistent with your words. Make sure your strategies are consistent with your philosophy.

That is another reason why effective NetWeaving must usually come after some level of maturity has been reached by the financial services professional. Anyone can put people together with other people but a true NetWeaver does some pre-screening to establish trust in the person(s) being matched as a problem solver or a resource provider. Becoming a trusted resource is not something that typically happens overnight.

Terri Gettman, J.D., CLU, ChFC, whom we met in Chapter One, has many of the characteristics that we have found in most of the NetWeavers we've interviewed. These individuals are genuinely interested in other people and go out of their way to help, often at their own expense, and often way above and beyond the call of duty. Integrity and honesty are very important and doing what's right and in the client's best interest consistently tops their list of what's most important.

Terri's career has been one mainly of support—acting as a resource to others—and making other people look good. That, in addition to her technical knowledge and creativity, is the reason agents, brokers and planners enjoy working with her so much.

Early in her career, when she was an advanced sales specialist inside an agency, Terri was working on a joint case with an agent whose prospect was a buddy in a breakfast club of which both were members. While Terri was reviewing the client's assets and documents as part of the financial planning review process, she discovered that what were supposed to have been qualified plan funds had not been properly set up and accounted for. Additionally, things looked suspicious in some other respects.

As she dug deeper, and as she and the agent brought what they were finding to the attention of an attorney who was also a member in the same club (without disclosing the name of the client, accountant or trust officer involved), they expressed their concerns. Ironically, as it turned out, the attorney was also representing another person who was involved in a similar set of facts and circumstances.

Consequently, he knew the parties without Terri ever having to break the pledge of confidentiality.

What finally came to light was that the accountant and trust officer were in cahoots with each other and they were raiding the funds from numerous accounts. What were supposed to be qualified retirement plans were never actually filed as such.

Obviously, Terri and the agent became heroes to the client involved as well as to the attorney. The client literally turned all his business over to them (buy-sell insurance, group, individual coverage, etc.) which, at its height, probably accounted for a quarter of the agency's entire production. That doesn't count any of the business subsequently referred to the agent by the grateful attorney.

NetWeaving Strategies

Global Stepping-Stones and the NetWeaver's Quilt

The concept of Global Stepping-Stones suggests that anyone you would want to meet or contact is only four or five people away from you. That means someone whom you know is familiar with someone who knows someone who can connect you with the person you want to meet.

That principle is exemplified by the saying, "It's a small world." There is a great probability that everyone you know knows someone with whom it would be of value for you to know. Some persons know a few hundred people while others know literally thousands.

NetWeaving takes a slightly different approach to the Global Stepping-Stones concept. Think of a quilt made up of four vertical and horizontal rows of patches (sixteen squares in total), all sewn together into one common tapestry, each different but each having a common thread. In other words, each person knowing the person who is represented by each adjoining square. The bottom right square represents the person you're trying to meet in order to add him to your resource bank or to match up with someone in a win/win relationship. Remember, you're not looking to *sell* him anything although, once he understands what you're all about, he may come seeking you or your services. You're looking to help him or to use his products or services to assist others in your contact network. You will also find the process of meeting him and getting others to introduce you much easier when he realizes that you have no ulterior motive other than to weave him into your NetWeaver's quilt.

As you look at the NetWeaver's Quilt diagram on page 48, notice there are many different paths that can be taken to connect the quilt squares in order to finally reach the person whom you are actually seeking to meet. Many times you won't know until later that someone can create an alternate path to reach the person with whom you are trying to contact. What's important is that you enter them in your mental resource Rolodex and that you have a clear picture of what they do so later you will be able to recognize that they might be the missing square of your NetWeaver's contact quilt.

Some Contacts Are of Special Importance

In your search for locating people who may be able to introduce you favorably to your new resource contact, be aware that there are a few power players out there who seem to know everyone. Many of those people are not power brokers, meaning they aren't in it for themselves. They just love introducing people to each other and putting people together. Those people are worth their weight in gold and when you meet one, you should take extra care to cultivate a relationship. Sooner or later, it will come back to benefit your search.

Wally Dale is a consultant these days, but for many years he was the most successful agency manager in the country for State

Farm Insurance. Out of 1,100 agencies, Wally's group led the company from 1985 to 1995. Wally is a natural-born NetWeaver. You almost never finish a conversation with Wally in which he hasn't told you about someone or something new in his NetWeaver's resource quilt.

One of Wally's most successful acts of NetWeaving, which has come back to benefit many of State Farm's agents across the country, was through a fellow manager, Jim Larsen. Wally had been on the lookout for a good estate planning attorney to help his agents with advanced cases. Although they had found many good attorneys over the years, it always seemed that at some point, they would bury them with business. Those attorneys either lost some of their sense of urgency, became too hard to reach or they simply moved on and were unavailable.

Through Jim Larsen, Wally was introduced to Mike Thiessen, an estate planning attorney in Kansas City, Missouri. Wally started asking Mike to help with cases in the Ft. Lauderdale area where Wally was based. On many occasions, Wally's agents would keep Mike busy for two days seeing their clients. In addition, Wally included Mike in planning meetings and referred him to other State Farm managers. After Hurricane Andrew, Wally took Mike into State Farm's home office and introduced him to the key people. Today, Mike and many of the 90+ attorneys in his office work with State Farm agents across the country, a tribute to Wally's NetWeaving years.

What a Wonderful World It Would Be

You know how automatic it is to talk about the weather with people. Instead, what if it was just as natural to talk about stepping-stones and your NetWeaver's Quilt? What if, during every conversation, you routinely talk with others to discover the commonalities of your interests or associations?

NetWeaving requires that you have a clear understanding of your quilt—where the contact points are and how you can fill in any missing swatches. At the same time you're approaching people with the thought of expanding your resource base for the benefit of others, you are also learning more about them, their needs, their problems, their ideas and their strengths and weaknesses. In other words, not only will global stone-stepping and NetQuilting strengthen your resource base, but each VIP you create in your network represents someone else whom you can link with others—creating value all around.

In the outmoded WIIFM (What's In It For Me) networking strategic approach, people are perceived as taking advantage of their networks of contacts in order to benefit themselves. At the other end of the networking spectrum, the WIIFY (What's In It For You) world—or in NetWeaver's lingo HCIHO (How Can I Help Others) approach—gathering resources, expanding your networks of contacts and filling in your missing stones or swatches is meant to benefit others more than yourself.

Just as it has been said that there is plenty of food to feed everyone on the planet, that it's just a matter of distributing the food into the right hands and eliminating the tremendous waste that goes on every day, so it is with NetWeaving. We have all these resources available to us—people and information—and there is no need to let them go to waste. Anything you could possibly want or need is around you—somewhere.

What is vital for making good use of those resources is an effective strategy. Where are the resources and how can we bring together the right parties? How can we locate and distribute the right resources and information to the right people? That's what strategic matchmaking is all about. That's the secret to NetWeaving.

Let's look at the NetWeaving diagram again.

Strategic Matchmaking

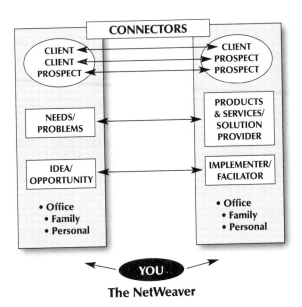

The NetWeaver

STRATEGIC RESOURCE PROVIDING

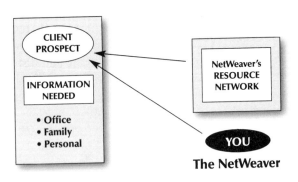

The NetWeaver

Strategic Matchmaking:
Matching up People With Other People

1. Product and service providers.

2. Problem solvers.

3. Idea/Opportunity Implementers, Enhancers, and Facilitators.

Strategic Resource Providing:
Matching up People With Resources or Information

1. Acting as the resource yourself.

2. Bringing in or referring to another resource provider.

3. Referring to an on-line source or resource.

If you were creating a NetWeaver's Yellow Pages, you would have General categories of people and resources and information that would be of value to anyone. The telephone number for the weather might be a perfect example.

Next you would have Specialist categories that are associated with your specialty. Your goal is to expand your value to the network by making yourself a more valuable resource commodity, both in your network of contacts as well as the information resources you bring to the table.

There are Resource and Solution categories; keep them separated by industry. Obviously, like the Yellow Pages, the list can be infinite so the idea is not to create a laundry list but to cover your bases in those major categories in which you want to concentrate as well as some general cross-purpose categories. It is also important to include a few of your very special interests that make you unique. Those might include an appeal for vintage autos, coin collecting, being a wine connoisseur, etc.

In reality, what happens is that as you approach people differently and as you ask yourself, "How can this person become a resource to some of my clients or prospects?" you will consistently discover interesting and valuable people who will become resources for you and your clients—and you for them—simply because you *asked*. Make sure to inquire about any special interests your clients or prospects might have. For example, I've been to parties where conversations uncover the fact that people who have known each other for years just happen to learn that they have a passionate avocation or hobby in common.

Here are some additional questions that can help you create your NetWeaver's Quilt.

- Who do I know who would be of value to this person in one or more of these areas?

- Who do I know who would be of interest to this person?

- Who do I know who would be a source of influence for this person?

- Who do I know who would be a prospect for this person's product or service?

- Who might this person know whom I would want to meet?

- Who do we have in common in our network?

- Who would be instrumental in helping us expand our relationship?

- What are the possibility and opportunity if we integrate our networks?

- What could we possibly do more effectively if we integrated our resources?

- What could we do to expand our reach and our resources?

- What could we do to expand our thinking?

- How could this person's idea fit in with my other contact's idea to strengthen both or to create a totally new concept or idea?

Four Easy Steps to Creating a NetWeaving Strategy

1. Establish and build your NetWeaving resource center—your mental Rolodex.

    - Keep Global Stepping-Stones and creating a NetWeaver's Quilt in mind.

2. Categorize your NetWeaving strategy by:

    - Matching people with other people:

        - Product/Service

        - Problem Solving

        - Idea/Innovation Implementer or Enhancer

    - Matching people with resources and information:

        - Acting as the resource yourself (General and Specialist categories).

        - Bringing in or referring to another resource provider for his or her information value.

        - Building a valuable resource library of Internet sites to supply to others.

In case you wonder what the difference is between matching persons with other persons in the Matchmaking category and matching someone with an information/resource provider, it is that the information/resource provider is agreeing to simply act as a free source of information to your party for a period of time. They are doing it because they believe in NetWeaving; they don't see it as giving away their services for free. Rather, it is a new business generation tool and a way to increase their value to you and to others in the network who will also be referring prospects and clients to them who actually need their services, not just some information.

In building your NetWeaving Yellow Pages, keep in mind the three contexts for each of the categories:

   a.   Business;

   b.   Family; and

   c.   Personal.

3.   Design a retrieval system that will facilitate easy access.

4.   Establish habits that will make NetWeaving a part of your daily life.

NETWEAVING
EXERCISE #3

Bob and Donna's Top 10 List of Ways to Become a Power NetWeaver

1. Always be on the lookout for NetWeaving opportunities; they are everywhere. All you need to do is train yourself to watch and listen.

2. Act as if *everyone's* problems are *your* problems...and *everyone's* opportunities are *your* opportunities. Learn to walk in their moccasins.

3. Become a good jigsaw puzzle solver. In other words, always look for ways to fill in more empty spaces in your Global Stepping-Stone chain and your NetWeaver's Quilt.

4. Be genuine and sincere in your NetWeaving, having the confidence to know that your matchmaking will come back to benefit you in many ways in the future. You need ask for nothing up front; your reward will come. If you charge for your matchmaking or resource services, remember to keep a clear distinction between those times when you are acting as a power broker and as a gratuitous NetWeaver.

5. Be creative in helping prospects and clients find ways to solve problems and ways to take advantage of opportunities. Try and associate with off-the-wall thinkers, especially if that's not your strong suit. Those people tend to challenge the status quo and "the way things have always been done." Wild-eyed brainstorming, with the brakes off, creates opportunities that many people are walking by every day and are missing. How about the guy with 3M who discov-

ered a glue that didn't stick very well although it ended up becoming what made Post-it®, Notes work?

6. Become a well-rounded reader if you are not already. Find some consolidated services such as the *Kiplinger Letter*, *Bottom Line* or *Executive Book Summaries* (short summaries of business books and articles). Also, if you are in even a medium-size to large city, there should be a business journal that will assist in your matchmaking and help you locate new and interesting resources.

7. Always be on the lookout for a charitable twist to your NetWeaving. That is a method to accomplish good deeds and get your client's business favorable publicity, or just favorable word-of-mouth PR, as a result.

8. Accept the fact that NetWeaving is a learned behavior that takes practice and more practice; it's not a natural activity for most people. Make it a daily habit.

9. Spread the word about the effectiveness of NetWeaving. The more NetWeavers there are out there, the better it is for *all* of us—and you'll get the credit for being a NetWeaving pioneer.

10. Remember that Power NetWeaving is following the Golden Rule: "Do onto others as you would have them do unto you"—but *you* be the first to NetWeave.

CASE STUDY: THE NETWEAVER'S QUILT

Backgrounds of the Players

This NetWeaving story perfectly exemplifies the benefits of both strategic matchmaking and strategic resource providing. It also just happens to involve three good friends of Bob Littell. Most of all, however, it shows how, just as a single stone thrown into a pond creates concentric circles of motion and activity which stretch far beyond the point of impact, a single act of NetWeaving can set a chain of events into motion that creates energy and activity far beyond the initial points of contact.

Bob started in the insurance business straight out of college in the late '60s with Fidelity Union Life by selling insurance to college students. After a fairly mediocre sales record but great success as an "expert" in joint work, he moved to the home office, first as head of advanced underwriting and eventually as a marketing vp. (At that point in his career, Bob described himself as too analytical for his own good.) The person in charge of training for the company was LaDale Young. Today, LaDale is a distribution vice president for Columbus Life.

Another friend to both Bob and LaDale is Bill Grubb who was a very successful regional vice president of the northeast region for Fidelity Union.

After leaving Fidelity Union, Grubb went with AIG (ALICO) as the executive vice president, marketing and agency, on an international basis until 1990. He then moved to become a partner and managing director of ICMS (InterContinental Marketing Systems). Today Bill, along with his partner and founder of ICMS, Terry Schuster, are managing principals of The Global Institute (TGI;

globalEDegree.com). The Global Institute has partnered with The American College, Life Underwriter Training Council (LUTC), Life Office Management Association (LOMA), The Million Dollar Round Table (MDRT), Kinder Brother's International, Financial Services Online (FSO) and several other content providers in order to create the first virtual on-line worldwide training organization.

The fourth person involved in this story is Bill O'Quin, co-creator and President of FSO (www.fsonline.com). His company, which has thousands of daily visitors from people in the financial services industry, provides weekly newsletters and E-zines covering industry news, marketing ideas and sales tips. Today, FSO is the largest distributor of web-based information to the financial services industry. Their inspirational DailyInBox.com e-mails are sent to 1.4 million people each day and their financial newsletters are received by nearly 60,000 a week.

Bill and his partner, Joan Barrett, a very talented writer and advanced underwriting expert, also created the Virtual Sales Assistant, an Internet-based resource for financial services professionals, and sold it to LUTC, now part of The American College. Joan has played an instrumental role in producing the quality industry news and other materials that have been used and enjoyed by many of us within the industry.

How It All Began

In the early '90s, O'Quin had taken early retirement from Prudential where he says B.B. Brown, another NetWeaving example in this book, taught him everything he knows. Back in his days at Prudential, Bill O'Quin worked with Joan whom he knew to be a great writer and subject matter expert.

By 1992, Fidelity Union had been acquired by Allianz. Bill O'Quin called on LaDale and said he needed to show him something. (O'Quin had first met LaDale through NetWeaving.) Acting as a strategic resource provider, Bill had volunteered his time to teach a General Agents and Managers Association (GAMA) course and met LaDale who was in the audience. They became close friends from that day forward. This was very early on, even before FSO was in existence. Most of what Bill had was boilerplate, although he envisioned that it would eventually be put on the Internet.

In 1995, Bill called LaDale but this time asked to meet him at the Bristol Suite Hotel. Again, Bill said he needed to show him something and to show him, Bill had commandeered the Bristol Hotel manager's office, including his telephone, and had hooked them up to the Internet. Remember, that was in 1995 when the Internet was still new stuff to most. LaDale admits he didn't understand everything he saw, but he saw enough that he advised Bill to take his ideas and make a go of it on his own because, in LaDale's words, "This is where everything's going to be going."

Three weeks later, O'Quin called LaDale and said, "If I fail, you know it's going to be your fault." With the blessings of his then boss and now CEO of the American General Life and Accident insurance Company, Joe Kelly, he resigned his position with American General, set up offices in Austin, Texas, and began a long process of trying to convince a skeptical financial services industry of where the Internet was going to be taking things.

Another Bill

About a year later, LaDale and his old friend, Bill Grubb, were walking down the hall at a Life Agency Management Program (LAMP) meeting when LaDale spotted Bill O'Quin. In true NetWeaver fashion, LaDale introduced the two Bill's and proceeded to explain why the two of them needed to become familiar with each another. Grubb didn't immediately appreciate everything he saw. Because he trusted and respected LaDale's opinion so much, however, he listened and kept coming back to learn more.

In 1998, while Bill O'Quin was still trying to open doors at various insurance companies, he and Bill Grubb had gotten to know each other well enough that they began to talk about some future partnering opportunities. Bill Grubb's company, ICMS, was and still is the exclusive distributor for LOMA and LUTC materials around the globe with sponsor relationships in fifteen countries. LUTC, with whom Bill was very close, along with Dennis Stork's insight and with help from Ed Morrow, one of the key contributors to the virtual marketing arm of FSO, saw an opportunity and decided to purchase FSO.

Bill O'Quin, while putting together all the various pieces of FSO, had also become a valuable strategic resource for Bill Grubb's company, ICMS. As Bill and his partner, Terry Schuster, began to grasp the potential for virtual training, especially in the rest of the world where they had already established a reputation for excellence through both LUTC and LOMA materials, the idea for The Global Institute was formed.

With Dr. Sam Weese, President of The American College, and Dennis Stork, President of LUTC, directing the integration of these two associations into one, it was only natural that this would give The American College strategic access to the NetWeaving relationships of ICMS, FSO, TGI and many others. Only the future will reveal the new NetWeaving experiences!

Lessons to Be Learned

There are many lessons in this case study. Not only does strategic matchmaking involve risks, but it can also create great rewards for those willing to take the risks. The NetWeaver's Quilt that was sewn by all the parties involved has now grown to include over a hundred people. This story is still a work in progress.

Another lesson revolves around the point that NetWeavers are able to accomplish more than others because by acting in their capacity as a gratuitous matchmaker and resource to others, they soon gain a level of trust which raises their stature, especially among their peers. When they speak, people listen.

Finally, it shows how both elements of NetWeaving—strategic resource providing and strategic matchmaking—blend and work together to further empower the NetWeaver.

chapter

5

BUILDING SUCCESSFUL
NETWEAVING HABITS

"We are what we repeatedly do. Excellence then is not an act; it is a habit."

– ARISTOTLE

If you've ever attempted to learn a new dance step, golf swing, tennis serve or musical instrument, you can probably remember how awkward it felt at first. However, over time and with practice, that golf swing or tennis serve becomes natural and consistent. Power NetWeaving™ is the same way. Connecting with others is mostly a learned behavior and learning anything takes repetition and practice. It is the repetition that creates consistency which fine-tunes one's skill, confidence and abilities.

It is, however, the nature of human beings for many of our habits—both good and bad—to become automatic. That's not necessarily bad, it's just the way it is. Yet, it can be bad if the habits we develop are unproductive or detrimental. Becoming a Power NetWeaver involves both shedding some of the bad or unproductive habits with which we've automatically become accustomed, as well as replacing them with new and productive skills and talents.

True champions in any field look like naturals because of their mastery of the skills that came from dedication, practice, focus and drive. Just as in sports, where there are "natural" athletes who seem to effortlessly learn to do what most of us have to work and slave at to perfect, so, too, it is with NetWeaving. There are those who NetWeave almost as second nature. Those NetWeavers can also benefit from reading this book, both by analyzing what they really do and how they do it, as well as looking for ways they can improve upon their natural NetWeaving skills.

For most of us, though, there is a learning curve to NetWeaving just like the one that comes with developing any new skill. We practice, learn from the practice, occasionally retrogress as we're learning and, if we stick with it and practice regularly, we finally perfect what we have learned. Unlike some habits which are short-term in duration, power NetWeaving is a very rewarding and enhancing process that will continue to enrich you and others around you throughout your life.

Forming a new habit or changing an old habit involves:

- Developing awareness;

- Being truthful with yourself;

- Practicing, repeating and reinforcing the new habit; and

- Structuring the maintenance support.

- Let's take an individual look at these four points.

Developing Awareness

The first step is to become aware of a habit you wish to develop or enhance, or an unproductive habit that you want to change, modify or eliminate. Things that we have done in the past that served us well might not serve us under current situations. Society has changed, the financial services industry has changed and we as individuals have changed. Therefore, it is unrealistic to think that the same habits and strategies that have worked for us in the past will continue to work for us in the future without any change.

Awareness is the first step to learning, growing or changing in any way. Awareness sheds light on a new way or new opportunity. Until we accept that we want to change in a positive way, or realize we are doing something that is unproductive or not as effective as it could be, we will continue to not know any better. Once we have awareness, then we have powerful choices.

It is easy in life to get into certain routines that become ruts. It is easy to get to a point in life and business where we start going through the motions. It can get to the point where we just take what comes our way rather than consciously directing our life.

Becoming aware that NetWeaving is a skill that you want to develop and eventually master is only half of it. The more difficult part involves an awareness of the attitudinal side of NetWeaving and an honest appraisal of your own values and beliefs. NetWeaving's foundation is partially based upon the premise that the most selfish form of self-promotion lies in promoting others. If giving, sharing and enriching others are not attributes you admire and consider worthy of being emulated, you should return this book and ask for your money back. Better yet, give it to a friend whom you know who gets turned on by these qualities.

Being Truthful With Yourself

It is important to be truthful with yourself about your habits—which ones are serving you and which ones are not. It is essential to be realistic and to be equally truthful with yourself about what you are actually willing to do to make changes in your life. Once you identify an unproductive habit ask, "Am I willing to do whatever it takes at this point in my life to make this change?" Don't give your energy to something that you have no passion for or commitment to alter. It is much better to tell the truth and, thus, concentrate on those things that you truly choose to impact.

As long as we are alive and alert, there will always be opportunities to grow and learn and develop new habits. Be brutally honest with yourself and choose to focus on what will serve you most at this point in your life and your business.

Only pursue this new paradigm if you sincerely fit the mold of a NetWeaver and you:

- are genuinely interested in helping yourself by enriching others.

- have a high degree of personal integrity in your dealings.

- get as much or more satisfaction out of watching others succeed as you do out of your own success.

- have the stamina and the resilience to understand that embracing these new attitudes and developing these new skills will take time and effort as well as a commitment to perpetual education and growth.

- are excited about learning how to connect people with people to create win/win relationships and see why it can become one of the most rewarding chapters in your life.

- are willing to accept the fact that NetWeaving carries risks and you are willing to take those risks.

Practicing, Repeating and Reinforcing the New Habit

Once you've been truthful with yourself, you will then have the energy and focus to make something happen. It will then be time to pick a new habit on which to focus. Oftentimes, people continue to focus on their unproductive habit with the thought, "I'm not going to do 'that' anymore!" In actuality, they are still focused on the unproductive habit. We cannot get rid of a habit by focusing on it and creating a vacuum. Your power comes from focusing on a *new* behavior or strategy until it becomes the new habit. Through focus, repetition and consistency, strategic matchmaking can become as automatic as shaking hands or driving a car.

We must learn to consistently ask strategic questions such as:

- Why, where, when and how could this person help someone else in my network or is this person possibly a future resource?

- Why, where, when and how could one of my current resources be of help to this person?

All of us develop habits from the time we are born. It's just that some of the ones we establish are *good* habits while some others are *bad*. Unproductive habits are most often formed as a result of *not* doing something, or doing something haphazardly or sloppily. Therefore, bad habits are typically formed by the *absence* of action, whereas good habits are almost always formed as the result of *consciously focusing energy* on a goal and sticking with it until the goal is achieved.

Discipline is required for forming almost any *good* habit, whereas *bad* habits are most often formed by the *absence* of discipline.

A good habit-forming goal can be more easily accomplished by breaking it down into smaller goals. Rather than a non-exerciser stating, "I'm going to run five miles this week," it would be better for that person to say, "I'm going to walk or run three days this week for at least twenty minutes." Once that attainable goal has been achieved and maintained for some period of time, a new, higher goal can be established. The key is to continue to reinforce the habit.

Fallbacks and relapses will happen. The question is not whether or not they will occur, but rather how the person reacts to the setbacks. If one takes the attitude of "I knew all along I couldn't do that," well, as Yogi Berra once observed, "It's déjà vu all over again."

For those who will show the discipline to pick themselves off the mat, the good news is that getting back to the point where you were when you fell short of establishing your good habit is much easier the next time around. Once you've reached a certain point, the brain remembers the route you took and you'll find it easier to return to the point at which you'd stopped growing. From there it's onward and upward.

Once any good habit has been ingrained into your behavior, it becomes fairly easy to maintain the optimum maintenance activity level. That's the good news. The bad news is that falling out of those good habits is not the nice, gentle slope that probably was responsible for developing the habit in the first place. Instead, it's more like falling off a cliff. Therefore, staying at your optimum maintenance activity level should be viewed as a tightrope. So long as the tightrope walker stays focused, maintaining his balance is a piece of cake. But if he looses concentration and focus, the drop is straight down to ground zero.

As we said earlier, the process of establishing good NetWeaving habits requires both embracing some attitudes involved with helping others while combining them with actual strategies that must be followed in order to accomplish your lofty objectives.

Much of the remainder of this book deals with how to establish and practice actual strategies that will enable you to build good NetWeaving habits.

Structuring the Maintenance Support

As we are developing a new habit, we need a support structure to remind us to practice that new habit consistently over a period of time until it becomes automatic. What will remind you to be a strategic thinker and a strategic matchmaker? What will remind you to always do favors for others? A support structure can be a buddy, a mental reminder, a record keeping system—automated or manual— or just a daily checklist.

NetWeaving can become a powerful habit in your life.

- What are you currently doing to generate NetWeaving activity?

- What more could you be doing to generate more activity?

- What current habits get in the way of your NetWeaving?

- What current habit(s) do you have which are most conducive to helping you become a power NetWeaver?

NETWEAVING EXERCISE #4

Building NetWeaving Habits

1. Find out what you have in common with others.

2. Learn to listen well to create the connection with others.

3. Think of someone every day for whom you can be or become a resource.

4. Meet someone new everyday and inquire about his needs and problems.

5. Call someone you barely know to offer her something.

6. Ask someone to introduce you to someone and then explain your win/win people connecting philosophy.

7. Call someone just to say hi. You'll be amazed at what often comes of it.

8. With every article or paper you read, think about whom you know who would benefit from reading it and to which one of your clients or prospects would you send it.

9. Learn to write notes on the back of someone's business card just after you've spoken with him or her. This will help you retain information that helps you be a strategic matchmaker.

chapter

6

DEVELOPING BETTER LISTENING SKILLS - A PREREQUISITE FOR BECOMING A POWER NETWEAVER

"Talk to a man about himself and he will listen for hours."

— BENJAMIN DISRAELI

As a kid gathered around a campfire, did you ever play the game where someone starts telling a short story and each person whispers what he heard to the person next to him? Remember how, as the story completed its way around the circle, so much changed that you didn't recognize the original story when it returned to the beginning?

For most of us, our listening skills are poor and our retention spans are pathetic. A power NetWeaver must make a dedicated effort to become a better listener and also to concentrate on finding ways to retain and better categorize information. That is crucial in order to retrieve it in a timely manner when the opportunity arises.

Here are some reasons why mastering listening skills is a must for the power NetWeaver:

- When you're listening, you're not talking and you are able to gather information.

- When you're listening, it's showing your interest in what the other person is saying. Since most people enjoy talking about themselves, especially about their accomplishments, they are automatically warming up to you as they talk. Consequently, they will be more willing to share their resources and their wisdom.

- Listening as a power NetWeaver means learning to listen with a different set of filters on. You're listening for needs, problems and opportunities with which you can assist. You're listening for *their* benefit…not yours.

- The better you listen, the more interesting you become. Everyone can be your personal mentor.

- The magic words that open up conversations are: who, what, where, when, why, how and how much.

Next is a list of tips for learning how to listen better as well as how to better retain the most important points.

- Rather than listening to retain entire sentences, listen for key words and memorize them. After you hear a key word or words, repeat it (them) to yourself several times.

  Memory experts suggest that the best way to remember a person's name is, after you meet the individual and hear his name for the first time, to associate in your memory the person's face as you repeat the name five or six times. Association and repetition are probably our two most important memory tools.

- Break down things you are trying to remember into groups of no more than three or four items. It's embarrassing but, for many of us, our memory span only stretches to three or four items or points. Why do you think telephone numbers are divided into two sets of threes and one set of four? For example, 404-555-1212.

  If you listen for key words, mentally group them into threes or fours and you'll be able to retain much more information and take better notes during and after your meeting.

- Even if you take good notes during a meeting, the sooner you rewrite your notes after the meeting the better and more thorough they will be. Failure to do so is the biggest mistake that people make. Some individuals carry pocket dictation recorders to facilitate retention. Systems will soon be commonplace that will allow you to record conversations with a handheld dictating machine onto a mini-CD. You will be able to return to your office, pop the disk into your CD-ROM drive on your computer and voilá, have an instant hard copy of your notes.

- Listen as if you are trying to determine what information will be included on your final exam.

In line with this, Bob raised a chuckle from Donna as he confessed how he had acquired his better-than-average listening and note taking skills. (Don't tell your kids this story.) When Bob was a sophomore in college, he made a bet with a friend that he could get by without buying his books that semester. He won the bet and went until his second semester during his senior year without buying his textbooks. Still, Bob pulled close to a B average. Bob stresses that his studies were in political science, psychology, sociology and not math or the sciences. Further, he would stay up the night before an exam and borrow someone else's books with which to review, but the lesson he learned is worth noting.

Bob went to *every* class and when he took notes, he was carefully listening for information that might become a good test question or a point that the professor would emphasize. That "selective" listening ability proved to be one of Bob's most valuable learning experiences of his entire college career.

- Listen and at the same time search through your mental Rolodex for a possible strategic match. Also, by thinking of an association with what you just heard, you'll retain the thought or the resource person's name better.

As mentioned before, word and concept association is one of our most powerful memory aids. Individuals who can memorize fifty people's names (or more) the first time they meet use an association helper of some kind.

First, they prememorize a list of items *in a specific order.* Let's say they go through five rooms of your house and memorize ten items (in order) in each room. For example, in your living room: 1) couch; 2) big easy chair; 3) rug; 4) coffee table, and so on. As these memory experts meet the people, they associate their name and face with the prememorized objects—Jan Smith sitting on the couch, Fred Jones in the big easy chair, Ted Allen sitting on the rug, etc. The prememorized list gives you a handle on which you can attach things you're trying to recall.

It's virtually impossible to be a power NetWeaver without being a good listener. Study other books on listening and commit to developing and improving better listening and retention skills.

NETWEAVING
EXERCISE #5

Developing Better Listening Skills

1. During the next conversation you have with a prospect or client, as you discuss their needs, problems, and interests, and after you are given a business card, write several key words on the back to help you retain important details you heard. Take another person's business card but, after a similar discussion, *do not* jot down any notes. After only a day or two, notice the differences in what you retain.

2. Repeat the first exercise but carry a little notepad (or pocket dictation machine) and take a few notes as soon as possible after your conversation with your prospect or client. Do not take any notes from any other conversation you have. Wait a day or two and attempt to recall as much as you can about both conversations and then notice the incredible difference.

chapter

7

NETWEAVING: CATEGORIES OF STRATEGIC MATCHMAKING AND RESOURCE PROVIDING

"In everyone's life, at some time, our inner fire goes out. It is then burst into flame by an encounter with another human being. We should all be thankful for those people who rekindle the inner spirit."

— ALBERT SCHWEITZER

The remainder of this book examines the "how to" of NetWeaving™ and will provide you with practical strategies for successful NetWeaving. Included will be more examples of how some of the most successful professionals in the financial services industry have achieved that standing during their careers. The text will also illustrate how, in many cases, NetWeaving has turned to reward them many times more than the effort it took up front.

NetWeaving, or matching up people in win/win relationships, could be categorized in any number of ways but we believe it can best be illustrated as shown next.

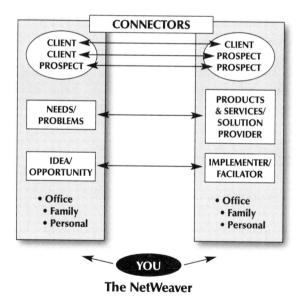

The NetWeaver

STRATEGIC RESOURCE PROVIDING

The NetWeaver

As you can imagine, there's an overlap among these three areas. That does not cause a problem because the idea is to cast your NetWeaver's net very wide in order to not miss any opportunities for being a strategic matchmaker or a resource provider to others.

For example, a client may tell you he or she has a need for some software to handle inventory control. Although you might not know anything about the best inventory control software, it just so happens that your mental Rolodex does contain the name of a computer guru whom you know and who previously managed a very profitable company. That person could be a valuable resource because he could:

1. recommend the appropriate software;

2. recommend that a person be hired to better manage the inventory because the software alone won't solve the problem;

3. recommend a company that could act as a part-time inventory control specialist or serve in that role himself.

The need for something other than just software could be categorized as an "unrecognized problem." Whichever the case, the important point is that you had a resource who could help either provide the product or service needed, or who could help solve the problem by supplying an information resource.

In the same situation, if you happened to be a software expert yourself (maybe not the case but humor us) and you not only could recommend a software program to use but could actually help install or instruct others on its use, then you could very well serve as the information source or resource yourself. In this particular example, *you* would be acting in all three capacities:

1. the product/service provider who finds the product and performs the service;

2. the problem solver who identifies the problem and who also provides the solution; or

3. the one who serves as the information resource provider.

It is important to understand that needs can be either "recognized" or "unrecognized." For all the obvious reasons, it's easiest to help fulfill needs when a person recognizes and admits he has a particular need for a product or service, problem solver, etc. This situation allows you to work on just one end of the connection.

On the other hand, some of the biggest rewards from successful NetWeaving occur when the need or needs are unrecognized or only partially recognized as in the previous example. Remember in that instance the person thought there was a need for inventory control software when, in fact, the real problem was much bigger. Your ability to help others see the true facts makes you even more valuable.

Your first job as a power NetWeaver is to help enlighten the individual as to why there is a particular need or problem. Sometimes, merely getting the client or prospect to talk about the need, problem, idea or opportunity might generate an idea for a possible resource you have in your mental Rolodex.

In other cases in which you can see the problem, but the client, prospect or friend can't (i.e., remember the story of the king who thought he was walking down the street wearing his newly created robe that was visible to all but him), you must use a great deal of creativity and statesmanship. You must somehow help the other person come up with the idea or solution you have in mind. If it's perceived as *your* idea, chances are slim he will take your advice. After all, what do you know about his business?

Finally, whether it is a matchmaking solution to locate a product or service needed, a problem for which a solution is needed, an idea or opportunity that needs some outside help, or finding a resource provider for information or resources that would be most useful, each NetWeaving opportunity can come up in a context of either the person's business, family or personal situation. This is true regardless as to whether they are recognized or unrecognized.

At a holiday party you introduce someone whom you know well to someone with whom you only have a passing knowledge. The person whom you know well is very interested in mountain climbing and, through someone else, you heard your newly introduced contact is also into mountain climbing. The introduction and drawing the topic toward mountain climbing was made purely as an act of socialization and friendship. When the two of them eventually become great friends as well as form a very successful business venture, they will obviously have a need for a variety of financial services. Guess who they will probably turn to first for help and advice?

The following chapters will examine the three main categories of connectors in more detail:

1.   Needs and Problems being matched with an appropriate Product or Service or Solution;

2.   An Idea or Opportunity that just needs the right fertilizer—expertise, money or both—to grow into a successful venture; and

3.   A need for Information that is satisfied either by the NetWeaver acting as the resource provider or by another person in the NetWeaver's resource Rolodex.

We'll explore these three categories within the contexts of business, family and personal needs.

Jack Baker, CLU, ChFC, AEP, is a consultant to McGriff, Siebels & Williams (MS&W), a property and casualty firm serving the southeast from Maryland to Texas. Jack also does a great deal of behind-the-scenes lobbying on a national basis for the insurance industry on tax issues, especially those relating to life insurance and charitable planning. He has become a master at being a strategic resource provider by building credibility with lawmakers and their staffs. He gives them a better understanding of the key issues and explains the complex ideas and concepts in ways they can understand. Jack helps MS&W with estate and charitable planning for their high net worth individuals and MS&W, in turn, helps serve Jack's clients with group benefits and property and casualty coverage.

Jack's relationship with MS&W has created opportunities for them to invent different p&c coverages and, in some cases, to obtain excess coverage that was not previously available. He has also acted as a creative resource for some of MS&W's clients by giving them ideas and planning opportunities about which they had never before heard.

One plus one often equals more than two and this type of NetWeaving proves beneficial to both sides of the equation. Always be on the lookout for symbiotic relationships where you can bring value to someone else's table, knowing that it will also work out for you in the long run.

We must stress that as the NetWeaving diagram shows, the movement between the two strategic matchmaking categories flows *both* ways. In some cases, the NetWeaver may be dealing with a person who has a particular need while you'll be searching your resources for someone who can supply the product or service which will satisfy that need. In other cases, you will be dealing with a product manufacturer or with a service provider and you, as a NetWeaver, will be looking to help him find a new customer for his product or service.

Obviously, if you can help someone be more successful selling more of his products or services, or if you lead a venture capital firm to a party with a prospective new idea opportunity, you will be performing one of the NetWeaver's most powerful functions.

CASE STUDY: NEW MEMBERS FOR THE RESOURCE TEAM

The financial services sector is changing character rapidly and clients are finding that the best advisors are providing them with services and resources that go far beyond the realm of the limited world they provided to in the past.

Several years ago, one of these missing services became very obvious to Bob, mostly as a result of co-developing *The Family Incentive Trust*™. It is a planning tool designed to deal with many estate owner's desire to transfer character incentives as part of the legacy he or she would leave to future generations rather than just financial assets.

What he and co-creator, Jeff Scroggin, noticed was that many of the estate and financial planning issues being considered, or which had already been put in place, would probably never have been implemented or would have blown up somewhere down the line. The reason is because all the advisors either ignored or never bothered to look into some significant dysfunctional family or business problems. A growing number of family business succession planning firms now focus *first* on those potential problem issues and put the planning second. Often those firms bring in, or have on staff, clinical psychologists who assist in taking those problem areas out into the open where they can be discussed and resolved. Therefore, in addition to adding a clinical psychologist to your NetWeaver's resource file, there are a host of other services that will become much more common in the future.

Troy Taylor, Managing Director of Source Capital South, LLC, works closely as a resource with General American agents and financial planners because of his investment background. His specialty is solving problems that medium to large-sized companies have including business value growth strategies, a lack of capitalization, unlocking trapped capital or refinancing or recapitalization, capital investment planning for expansion, buyouts and much more.

In one such situation several years ago, Troy was brought in to help a value priced retailer that was earning over $50 million in annual sales. For years, H.M., the founder of the company, and his son-in-law, C.P., who was running the show along with help from the founder's son, J.M., discussed merger possibilities between themselves and a competitor who operated in different markets. There were no dysfunctional family problems and the son and son-in-law got along great. The real problem was that the other competitor was twice as large as their firm and they didn't like the idea of being swallowed up. The issue was forced to a head when the other company made a cash offer. At that point, Troy was brought in to explore the alternatives.

The two sides ended up structuring a transaction whereby H.M.'s company was sold to a financial group (Troy's company took a piece as well) for an amount that exceeded what the competitor had offered. C.P. and J.M. retained a significant ownership interest and the deal also included a considerable cash component for the family, including C.P. and J. M. Six months later H.M.'s old company acquired the other company and made C.P. the CEO of the combined companies. Together, then, they earned in excess of $200 million in sales making them one of the country's largest retailers in that industry.

chapter

8

NEEDS AND PROBLEM CONNECTORS— PRODUCTS AND SERVICES/ SOLUTION PROVIDERS

"A problem well-defined is a problem half-solved."

— EARL NIGHTINGALE

Putting people who have *needs* for specific products or services together with people who can *provide* those same products or services, or putting people who have *problems* together with people who have *solutions* to those problems, are both the most obvious and oldest forms of NetWeaving™. That strategic matchmaker role has been going on since the beginning of commerce and trade. Those who learn to excel at those skills are not only some of the most highly sought after individuals, but they achieve higher status and higher incomes because their network of contacts and influence makes them such a valuable commodity.

As mentioned in Chapter 7, NetWeaving goes both ways and sometimes the NetWeaver starts out on the Needs and Problems side seeking to help someone locate products, services or solutions. On other occasions, the NetWeaver works with someone on the supply side who is looking for more customers or someone who offers solutions to problems. The job placement business offers a perfect example of the bi-directional nature of NetWeaving.

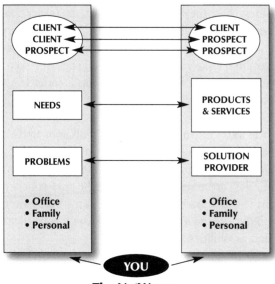

The NetWeaver

Looking at the situation from the viewpoint of the NetWeaving diagram, individuals looking for a job have a need and a problem. They have both a need for a new job and a problem—no job. On the other side of the diagram are the companies looking to hire people. They are looking for qualified candidates to fill openings or new positions.

There are two types of companies operating in the job placement business: placement firms and search firms. Both of them are acting as professional NetWeavers or strategic matchmakers.

Job placement firms or employment agencies serve those individuals who go to them seeking help in finding a job. The firms will make inquiries to companies on behalf of their clients, send out blanket resumes and do everything possible to place a job candidate in a new position. From the NetWeaving diagram perspective, those placement firms are acting as a professional NetWeaver by serving people who have both a need—no job—and a problem—being matched up with a company that can supply a job.

Executive search firms are in the same professional matchmaking business but they are working on the other side of the NetWeaving diagram. Like placement firms, they are also in the business of placing people in jobs, but their client is the company seeking to fill a position, usually at a very high level. They will often seek suitable candidates among individuals who, until contacted, were perfectly content where they were.

You, as a strategic matchmaker, might occasionally be able to do the same thing either a placement company or a search firm could, depending upon whom you are representing. If you have a client who is out of a job or between jobs, you might raise your antennae to determine if you know of anyone in the same business or industry who might be looking for a new employee with your client's qualifications and capabilities.

On the other hand, your client might be a business owner who tells you he or she is looking for a high level candidate to fill a certain opening. You might propose a meeting with a friend, client or prospect who wasn't even looking but who would be flattered and intrigued by talking about the opportunity.

We hope you can now clearly see the bi-directional way you can be a NetWeaver, remembering that your NetWeaving can be done in a business, family or personal context. As an example, it can be argued that helping someone locate or buy a new home impacts all three: the business, the family and the person.

Matching People with Products and Services to Offer With People Who Have Needs and Problems

Doug Hesse, CFP, Atlanta, Georgia, is consistently listed as one of the *Atlanta Business Chronicle*'s top 20 financial planners. Doug is NetWeaving all the time. Detailed next is one instance that exemplifies both the power of NetWeaving in helping a client find a new home as well as helping a realtor generate more business.

Two of Doug's friends were looking to move to the same development where he and his wife, Ro, own a lake home. Instead of simply recommending a realtor and providing the telephone number of the person who had done such a good job for him, Doug went along to introduce both parties. Although he wouldn't say so, Doug's presence probably did as much to help close the sale as the realtor's experience. The end result was that Doug's friends were extremely grateful that he spent the better part of two days with them and the realtor. As a sign of appreciation for Doug's involvement, the realtor returned the favor by asking Doug to help with his own financial planning in addition to introducing him to another strong financial planning candidate. As we have shown through previous examples, Doug's experience illustrates that NetWeaving often means just going that one extra step.

NetWeaving in a Business Context

Most of us have personal or business relationships with some realtors, travel agents, car dealership owners or salespeople and, assuming a trusted relationship has been established, a power NetWeaver can become a never-ending source of business for them.

LaDale Young, a regional vice president for Columbus Life, has probably sold more Cadillacs for his friend who owns the local dealership in Dallas than some of the dealership's own salespeople.

If you are working with a client or prospect who is selling a product or a series of products, you should first find the answer to their 80/20 secret—eighty percent of almost everyone's business comes from twenty percent of their customers. The secret, therefore, is what do those twenty percent look like? As your client or prospect describes his best customers, often a name or two will pop out of your NetWeaver's mental resource Rolodex.

Now, of course, you can make some NetWeaving points if you help add another customer to your client's business even if it is on the less profitable end. However, if you focus on the end that is most profitable to them (the twenty percent end), that is where adding another client to their list will generate for you the most points as well as help you build and reinforce your status and reputation as a power NetWeaver.

Next are a few hints on what you should do and what you need to know in order to become an effective NetWeaver.

- Understand the nature of your clients' or prospects' business. Where and how do they make their money? Stay at that until you can recap what they do and how they have become successful.

- Be able to summarize your clients' or prospects' business in an "elevator statement." It is called an elevator statement because you will typically have just a short time to explain to someone your clients' or prospects' business in order for them to visualize if there is a possible strategic fit with what they need.

• If your clients' or prospects' sell a series of products or services, you should understand which are the most profitable and who their best prospects are for those products or services.

• How did your clients or prospects land their largest accounts and from where do their best customers originate? As they are talking, do any names of current resources in your mental Rolodex come to mind?

• Do your clients or prospects have target companies or accounts they would most like to acquire? Do they have prospects to whom they would most like to sell? Make notes of their comments and put them into your NetWeaving client contact resource tracking system. In other words, fill in one of your Global Stepping-Stones or a missing patch on your NetWeaver's Quilt.

• Who are your clients' and prospects' major competitors? Where are they stronger than their competition and where are they weaker? Identifying where they perceive they are weaker might open up an opportunity for you to identify a service provider who can eliminate or offset a weakness they have.

• What do they see as the three biggest obstacles standing in the way of doing substantially more business than they are doing currently?

Here are more suggestions an advanced NetWeaver might look into.

- Help get a favorable article published about the company, the product or the service by matching up a reporter with the client.

- Be aware of whether your client or prospect would want to be in a position to *acquire* another company or *be acquired*, providing the price were right. Top NetWeavers have contacts who are business brokers who are always looking for those kind of situations, especially with a family owned business that has good cash flow and no obvious heir apparent.

If your business client or prospect is a service related company, many of the same questions apply but we've found that most of their problems will relate to simply finding more customers. Most of their needs, other than finding more customers, relate to running their business more effectively and efficiently. Keep those points in mind when dealing with any service related business.

NetWeaving With Other Financial Service Professionals

What should be the most natural form of NetWeaving—matching up your prospects and clients with other members of the allied professions—just doesn't happen often enough. Lack of trust, combined with a concern that something could go wrong that would reflect poorly on their existing relationship, is typically cited as the number one reason more professionals don't engage in it more often. The second most mentioned reason is a simple lack of awareness.

Tony Gordon, President of the Million Dollar Round Table for 2001, and the first MDRT president from outside North America, commented as to why he thought allied professionals don't do more NetWeaving. He proposed that the principal reason is a lack of confidence suggesting that members say to themselves, "I don't know enough about accountancy or business or law…or, what if after I put them together they don't like each other?"

These professionals mistakenly worry that if things don't work out the client will say, "It's your fault." Tony responded, "We hold back from helping people which could pay dividends in the future."

Tony's main suggestion, though, applies both to working with allied professionals as well as to how we NetWeave with our clients. Tony advises stepping back and asking ourselves a simple question: "Do we take the lead and offer referrals ourselves?" Many of our clients, he says, are looking for new clients for their business or profession. When did *we* last give a referral to a client?

To change that attitude Tony offers that when we are going through a client's file prior to a meeting, we should not only ask, "What new business can I sell (or new service can I offer)?" but also, "How can I help my client? Who can I think of to give my client as a referral?"

Tony points out there are two benefits to asking those questions. First, it's hard for someone who has received referrals from you not to reciprocate when asked. Secondly, when a client succeeds in doing business with someone we referred, it works wonders with our confidence. It puts us in a position of being able to NetWeave confidently.

NetWeaving seems to occur most often in those situations where there is almost a constant stream of referrals going back and forth between or among allied professionals. It also happens where such a trusted relationship exists that both or all of the professionals are convinced they are doing their client a huge favor by introducing the other professionals into their life.

What can people in any of the professions do to increase their NetWeaving activities? Here are some options.

- Find the best and brightest among other professionals and build relationships with them. Constantly be on the lookout for new stars of whom you were unaware who work in your own backyard. Let them know of your expertise and your interest in NetWeaving.

- There's a restaurateur in Atlanta who is also a radio personality named Ludlow Porch. One of Ludlow's classic, catchy ad slogans is, "Come see us. You gotta eat lunch somewhere...and we need the business."

- Become an active member of your local estate planning council, the planned giving council or form a study group made up of allied professionals who have a similar interest or purpose, such as employee benefits or retirement planning.

- Lead the way. If everyone tried to become the first one to be the strategic matchmaker, all of the professions would need to grow to meet the increased demand.

- Join the Society of Financial Service Professionals (SFSP) and become a member of one or more practice specialties that exchange information on-line. You'll find a wealth of experts with whom you can NetWeave long distance or in person.

As you become a power NetWeaver, you will find joy in building powerful relationships among a wide-range of professionals.

The Greatest Power NetWeavers Are Never in Need of More Business

The best power NetWeavers usually have more business than they can handle because it's coming to them from every direction. In fact, they are sending business back the other way as well.

Two of Bob's friends in Atlanta, Jeff Scroggin, J.D., LL.M., and Doug Duncan, J.D., LL.M., are two of the best NetWeaving attorneys

Bob knows. Consequently, partly due to their knowledge and excellent reputations which they combine with their NetWeaving prowess, they are in the category of never having to go looking for more business.

One of my favorite statements about NetWeaving as it relates to work among the allied professionals came from Jeff Scroggin. "Over the years, it has been amazing to me how so many of my professional relationships have turned into close, personal relationships and the open hand kindness that so often results from those personal and professional relationships. One adage of my practice has always kept me in good stead: I do not represent people I do not like personally. Because I generally like them, long-term clients tend to become personal friends, especially when we discuss so many intimate areas of their life."

In one of those situations, Jeff was brought in by a CPA (whom he had known for years) to assist with the CPA's client who had a growing business but which was experiencing significant cash flow problems. Lenders did not want to make any loans to the business and, although the CPA was doubtful the business could survive, recommended that the client declare bankruptcy. Jeff, who was also a CPA by training, suggested that the company should try and stick it out for a few more months to determine if they could extend their accounts payable. Jeff talked with the business owner every week or so during his struggle and gave him the cheerleading support he needed. Several years later, his friend, once on the verge of bankruptcy, sold his business in a pre-IPO roll-up that could earn him $6 to $8 million.

Incidentally, Bob and Jeff and the business owner not only have a business relationship, but they became skiing buddies and trusted family advisors. In Jeff's mother's words, "All you have at the end of your life that matters are friends and family." NetWeaving is not about making money, it's about making relationships. The money will take care of itself.

NetWeaving in a Family or Personal Context

Just as in the case above, NetWeaving in a business context often pours over into a family or personal context. That just comes naturally for many NetWeavers. Questions that often arise are "What would make this person's life or situation better?" "What would make either his family or his own life more secure, more prosperous, more well-rounded and peaceful, with less stress and conflict and with fewer problems?"

Perhaps the most obvious example of this, which also crosses over into all three contexts of business, family and personal relationships, is when a client or prospect of yours loses his job, or is not satisfied with his current position and is looking for a new opportunity. A skilled and experienced NetWeaver might do any of the following.

- Help his client or prospect fine tune his resumé (e.g., show the prospect where to go on the Internet for tips).

- Be on the lookout through his contact network, as well as in business journals, etc., for the job description matching the talents and skills of his client or prospect.

- Volunteer to act as a reference, assuming the client or prospect would consider that to be helpful, providing the NetWeaver feels comfortable in making a positive recommendation.

- Develop relationships with some headhunters or executive search firms, especially if the NetWeaver's market consists largely of corporate executives.

- Cultivate relationships with some outplacement firms, especially those who help outsourced, middle-aged executives, managers and supervisors maintain a positive mental attitude when they may feel they are "over the hill" or that their skills are outdated.

- Have some knowledge of the Consolidated Omnibus Budget Reconciliation Act of 1985 (COBRA) in order to advise clients and prospects about their rights.

- Build on relationships with psychological testing firms that might be able to help direct his client or prospect to a field possibly better suited to his talents and interests.

- Send out a copy of his client's or prospect's résumé to some contacts within his network and make some followup calls to determine if there is a match between the talents of the client or prospect and the needs of a would-be employer.

- Recommend books or motivational tapes (or provide them himself) or support groups on the Internet to help the client or prospect maintain a positive attitude.

- Recognize the stress that comes with these situations, especially on the home front, and be willing to genuinely act as a sounding board or shoulder to cry on if the client or prospect needs either or both.

Bev Brooks, whom we met in Chapter 3, told us a story that perfectly exemplifies how NetWeaving does not have to be anything more than helping out someone in a very simple way.

It happened almost twenty years ago while Beverly was still in an insurance company home office position. It involved a dynamic woman in Beverly's community whom she had met who was responsible for the marketing efforts within her family-owned and operated architecture firm. Beverly was very impressed with the woman and offered to sponsor her for membership into the Executive Women of Dallas, an organization made up of the female movers and shakers. About two years after the initial introduction, as Beverly was breaking out on her own, her now good friend went to her and asked how she could assist with Beverly's new career. Beverly responded by asking her friend if anyone was handling the firm's employee benefits. Beverly was told they had a plan but no agent. Beverly became the agent of record and the twenty person firm eventually grew to over 250 employees with offices in multiple states. As you might guess, there were many other insurance needs to be taken care of. Perhaps of greatest satisfaction to Beverly is that, when other agents come calling, the firm won't even talk with anyone else. The standard response is, "Beverly Brooks handles *all* our insurance needs."

The more you NetWeave, the luckier you get.

A Personal Story

Nearly twenty years ago, co-author Bob Littell was in the process of leaving an insurance company home office position in Dallas to move to Atlanta to spearhead the marketing for another insurance carrier. After having accepted the new position, and within weeks of moving to Atlanta, Bob received a call from a headhunter about another chief marketing officer position that had opened up in Texas. This position offered more money and a possible shot at the presidency within a few years. It was very tempting but Bob felt obligated to stick with his commitment to the Atlanta company.

Nevertheless, he contacted someone at his former company whom he knew to be unhappy with the situation and who was beginning to look for other opportunities. Bob asked for a copy of the individual's résumé and sent it to the headhunter along with a letter of introduction and recommendation.

That person was offered and accepted the position where today he is president of the company. That person has since referred several other key people within the company to Bob, some of whom later departed to form companies of their own, and on whom Bob has written significant amounts of life insurance as well as disability income insurance. Today Bob continues to NetWeave with his network of contacts within his expanded NetWeaver's Quilt.

Align Yourself with a Techno Guru

The best NetWeavers are always trying to "walk in the moccasins" of their best clients and most promising prospects. One way to be a true hero is to help them recognize the need for a product or service that can make their business more profitable or more efficient. Your prospects and clients are often too caught up in the daily grind to take the time to also be in the research and development business. Many of these missed opportunities are related to new technologies, equipment or software that could make the business more profitable.

Making some strategic connections with plain talking techno gurus who will be your eyes and ears for what's out there, or what's going to be out there within the near future, can make a huge difference. It should be noted that care is needed so you don't put unknowing clients or prospects, yourself included, on the bleeding edge rather than on the leading edge. A good way to determine that is by watching how the consultant runs his or her own business. If he or she is always buying the latest toys and wants you to do the same, proceed with caution. On the other hand, when you find someone who has given you great advice over an extended period of time and is consistently finding ways to keep current but spending *your* money as if it were his or her own, then you have found a great service provider and resource.

A few examples of NetWeaving along those lines include:

•   Matching up a client or prospect with someone who can provide that product or service that you think *might* supply your client or prospect with a competitive edge that he has not determined on his own.

•   Identifying one or more techno gurus who are proven entities, both in their abilities to save you money when purchasing products (e.g. buying computer systems and equipment) to how they can serve as your eyes and ears for technologies that are now applicable but not yet widely known.

- When you become a key matchmaker for your techno guru expert, you not only move up on his priority list when problems arise that need a quick fix, but your bill tends to be lighter when you are a source of referrals.

The Need for a CFO or a Strategic Coach

Many successful businesses reach a plateau from which they don't seem able to escape and they can't figure out why. In many cases, what's really needed is an outside creative, strategic coach who can not only help identify opportunities that the business owner might be missing (often right under his nose), but be able to develop some financial strategic moves that can free up capital for expansion, help fund new acquisitions, decide how to best expand the business, etc.

The problem is that many companies in that position and at that level don't feel they have the resources to afford a full-time chief financial officer. Fixing the problem is not a function for a bookkeeper even though the company might have a very talented CPA who does the books and prepares tax returns. No, the role we are outlining is really for a financial strategic coach.

There is a growing industry of these individuals, many with large accounting firm backgrounds, who are acting simultaneously as part-time CFOs for a number of companies. They bring in fresh ideas and they can often share strategies which they have seen successfully applied elsewhere.

A first class NetWeaver might do any of the following:

- Identify a couple of firms in the area that are now specializing in this area for strategic matchmaking purposes.

- Even in a small community, NetWeavers can suggest to some strategic minded, creative CPAs to start up such a practice.

- Line up meetings with clients or prospects who might have plateaued (as described above) and who might find this option to be just what they need.

NETWEAVING
EXERCISE #6

Developing Relationships With
Techno CFOs and Strategic Coaches

1. How many relationships do you have with people who supply products or services that your clients and prospects could use? What is your relationship with your automobile dealer, automobile mechanic, techno guru, CFO, strategic coach, or travel agent?

2. When was the last time you acted in a NetWeaving capacity, in either direction, by matching a client who had a need or problem with the product or service or solution provider? When was the last time you helped match someone on the supply side?

3. Do you have relationships with other financial services professionals in which you regularly send business back and forth? If yes, could you do more of it? If no, why not?

chapter

9

IDEA OR OPPORTUNITY CONNECTORS— CONNECTORS— IMPLEMENTERS AND FACILITATORS

"The optimist sees opportunity in every danger; the pessimist sees danger in every opportunity."

– SIR WINSTON CHURCHILL

Many people who are the most creative are not necessarily good detail people. They are considered right brain thinkers and that gives them a big advantage when it comes to dreaming up new ideas or having the ability to see things that other more logical thinkers might miss (the Hula Hoop, the Pet Rock). However, they face a major disadvantage when it comes to implementing their idea or making a business out of a great idea. Sometimes they also mistakenly believe the whole world thinks and operates the same way they do and, consequently, they often have many blind spots.

Some of these individuals are stubborn and think they can do it all, or at least do it with just a little help. Others are willing to admit their weaknesses and would jump at the opportunity of finding those with strengths in the business details (i.e., strategic marketing, financials, venture capital, etc.). A skilled NetWeaver might have just the right resource in his NetWeaver's Quilt who either could partner with such a person or, more likely, know someone who might make the perfect match.

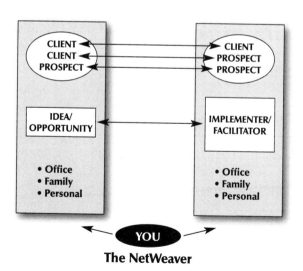

The NetWeaver

In spite of the opportunities available with that high risk/high payoff form of NetWeaving™, we must start this chapter with a warning. Every NetWeaving matchup, similar to the Clark McCleary example in Chapter 1, that places a neighbor looking for a job with another contact does not always work out successfully.

Of the two strategic matchmaking categories of NetWeaving, putting someone who has an idea or opportunity together with someone who can help implement it, or at least facilitate or enhance it, holds the greatest opportunity for fantastic success. It also encompasses the greatest possibility for abject failure and finger-pointing: "Why did you ever suggest this or why did you ever introduce me to so and so?"

A case in point. Bob has an attorney friend who told him a NetWeaving story that reinforces what we have said about the downside of NetWeaving. The account illustrates the risks involved when the NetWeaver puts together business people.

Bob's friend had a client who was one of those driven, workaholic individuals who couldn't delegate; he had to do everything himself. The stress accumulated and he paid the ultimate price when he suddenly died of a heart attack. Instead of selling the business then and there, the widow attempted to keep the business going. Within a short period of time, the business was worth substantially less than what it had been when it was a going concern.

The attorney happened to have another client who owned a business that was tangential to his deceased client's industry. Since this other client was a very astute businessman, the attorney decided he would at least make an introduction and see if they had enough interests in common to form an alliance. They did come together and the individual did help turn things around and then found a buyer for the deceased gentleman's company. Unfortunately, a friend of the widow convinced her that the business was worth many times more than what she received and the attorney ended up being sued for malpractice. Although the attorney won the case, it was a very expensive and professionally negative experience. Would he do the same thing, had he to do it all over again? Absolutely, he said. NetWeavers act because they believe in the worth of their strategic NetWeaving and accept the risks that come with it.

To see it from another point of view, there is no difference in coming across someone who just had a heart attack. Even though you administer CPR and mouth-to-mouth resuscitation, the individual still dies and the family of the deceased sues you. Although there will always be risks when you perform good deeds, they will pale in comparison to the rewards.

In the vast majority of cases, even if a new venture does not work out or doesn't work out as well as initially expected, it's rare that the party or parties will fault the NetWeaver. Most people assume the responsibility for the decision and the outcome even if it doesn't turn out favorably while the NetWeaver is still considered a valuable resource. There are occasions when a NetWeaver will adopt the attitude, "If at first you don't succeed, try, try again" and it might be the second or third attempt before things finally click.

As you know, the track record for new businesses is not great and the majority do not succeed over time. That is also true for companies who undertake a major departure from what they've done successfully. Some of the most successful businesses are those who "stick to their knitting" and don't stray too far from what they know best. On the other hand, the saying, "No guts...no glory" also means that for the few who do dare to wander beyond the boundaries of comfortability and blaze the uncharted path, the rewards can be the greatest. In today's rapidly changing environment, "business as usual" doesn't carry the same assurances it once did. In today's atmosphere, the business that continues to operate the way it has always operated can find itself in serious trouble in a relatively short period of time.

Use the following questions up front to gauge whether your NetWeaving has a decent chance for success.

• Do the two parties have the necessary tools to get the job done?

It's one thing to have a great idea. Most ideas or innovations will not succeed in their original form and need a little morphing. Therefore, the idea or innovation initiator must be flexible enough to realize that and accept outside input even if it means substantially changing from the original concept. Stubbornness and inflexibility by the creative party, the inventor or innovator is a recipe for failure.

In the same way, the business or financial person may have *some* of the tools necessary to help put the business end of things together. Yet, if he or she doesn't recognize and admit his or her own limitations, things can also go wrong. Many people who are good on the financial or bookkeeping side of a business, and who often have good computer knowledge and skills as well, are not always terrific on the strategic thinking side. It is those business people who can be matched with a creative CPA who specializes in business strategic planning, or with one of a growing number of part-time CFOs who take on a handful of clients whose businesses have not yet reached a point where they can justify a full-time CFO position. Many of those people have large consulting company backgrounds and have chosen to go out on their own. That can be a great match.

•   Do the parties have the financial resources to launch the venture or do they have access to sufficient capital?

Most new businesses fail because they run out of money. Many are inside the ten yard line when it happens but they can't score. Many entrepreneurs go into business with the naive belief that, "If you build it, they will come." They just assume that when the product is built or when they start offering the service, people will beat down their door to buy the perfect mousetrap. They also suppose that somehow, when the idea is launched, some financial guardian angel will see the worth of the idea or innovation and bail them out or buy them out for ten gazillion dollars. Sometimes a bail out will occur, but when it happens the angel is often the one who walks away with the great deal. At that point, the original business owner probably would not use the word "angel" to describe his rescuer(s).

Usually, rescuers cannot be found in time and the buyouts are few and far between. Unless the parties are committed and have the financial staying power (or have access to it), chances for success are very dim. You, as the NetWeaver, would be safer to either avoid those situations altogether or be very forthcoming with the parties and indicate that you are skeptical about their chances without better financial backing.

- Are these nouveau entrepreneurs committed to staying lean in the early years, or do they enter into the enterprise with a *big company* mentality?

Many new businesses are being started by people who have retired in their early or mid-50s or early 60s and who are funding their startup with their retirement nest egg generated from their large company retirement plan.

Business people who start up with a big company mentality and spend money as if it wasn't theirs (justifying it because they believe they must think, look and act big to become big quickly) usually find it doesn't always work that way. It always takes much longer than they think it will and it always takes more money. Thinking and acting small and spending frugally from day one will not only conserve the scarce resources it takes to operate a business but, with the technology that is available today, it's possible to operate a company at a fraction of what it used to cost as long as the people are smart and manage their resources carefully.

Once again, where you sense the party(ies) for whom you're trying to be the matchmaker have the big company mentality, you are probably wise to pass on them or attempt to get them to see the wisdom in starting lean and mean.

When one of those businesses does make it, as in Clark McCleary's story, there is tremendous satisfaction in having helped create something that is benefiting the whole economy—jobs for all the people employed by the business. It can also be like watching a child grow to become a responsible adult and the pride that comes from being able to look back and see the part you played up front to help make it all possible.

Jeff McCart, CPCU, ARM and vice president of McCart Insurance and Risk Management, Inc. in Duluth, Georgia, suggests that NetWeaving is one of the most important components of what he offers his clients.

Well over a year ago, Jeff was introduced to Ernie R. Bonistall, president of The Right Call, Inc., a telecommunications auditing service company. The purpose of the meeting was for Ernie to make a proposal to review McCart's telecommunication services for his company. If the audit proved successful, Jeff was told that his company could probably recoup a minimum of $2,000 to $5,000 in savings and The Right Call would make approximately the same amount as a fee for its services.

After listening to Ernie's presentation, Jeff told him he wasn't interested in the audit at that time. However, he was impressed enough with what he saw that he volunteered to share his opinions, along with one of Ernie's brochures, with one of the McCart company's major clients. On March 23, 2000, The Profit Recovery Group International, Inc. acquired Ernie's company for about $5.5 million.

Unfortunately, Jeff never heard so much as a thank you from Ernie but offered, "My whole practice has been performing NetWeaving. We do it because it's part of our corporate culture and because we believe in it as just another one of those services which we provide our clients, not because we're looking to gain something from it. Most of these [NetWeaving opportunities] will come back around to benefit us in one way or another. But even when one doesn't, we still have the satisfaction of having served a client in a way few others would have attempted to do."

chapter

10

INFORMATION NEEDED
CONNECTORS -
RESOURCE PROVIDERS

"Genius is one percent inspiration and ninety-nine percent perspiration."

– THOMAS EDISON

There is no question that some people are much better than others at becoming *great* strategic matchmakers—putting people together in win/win relationships. Whether it's putting people who have problems, needs, ideas or innovations together with those who can solve problems, fill needs or implement ideas, or going in the other direction with those who supply or serve the ones in need, the relationship enhancement aspect of NetWeaving™ seems to be more difficult for some than for others.

Realistically, not everyone will become a power NetWeaver from a strategic matchmaking standpoint. Anyone and *everyone*, however, can become a great NetWeaver from a strategic resource provider standpoint.

STRATEGIC RESOURCE PROVIDING

The NetWeaver

We all have a thirst for information. The trouble is there's just so much to learn and so little time in which to learn it. Often, the information we need the most is the information that we don't even realize we need. Therefore, we must rely on others to be a resource in those important areas where we are weak as well as to point out information that will be of great value, but of which we are not even aware.

A power NetWeaver, by definition, is someone who is a great information resource on a variety of subjects. We must point out that it is not necessary for the NetWeaver to be the fountain of knowledge himself, only that he has *access* to resources who can supply the answers to questions or just provide meaningful data.

Think of the name of the first person who comes to mind whom you would characterize as a veritable walking encyclopedia of information on virtually any topic. That individual seems to be a real-life *Jeopardy* player who knows everything from meaningful and useful information to seemingly trivial but interesting information. You wonder how anyone could have enough time to absorb so much information and have it all available at an instant. Those people are few and far between.

Well, the Internet has changed all of that. Most everyone can now sound and perform like a genius simply by knowing how to search the web and retrieve information on virtually any topic.

In order to become an expert information retriever, you no longer must spend hours surfing the web to find the best sources because there are companies, primarily e-based companies, that do the work for us. World Best Websites (www.worldbestwebsites.com) lists the sites that are best for surfing the net. They are one of a growing number of sites which are focusing more on filtering and prioritizing the information. By filtering we mean that the person gets to choose the information he *doesn't* want to see in order that he doesn't waste a lot of his time sorting through information and resources that are of no interest. By prioritizing information that is based upon a person's individual tastes and desires, you are showing that which is of greatest interest first and allowing the user to disregard the rest.

One of those players, www.gomez.com, does a good job of ranking items in a number of categories in order to help you inform your prospects and clients about where to go for the best products, services and information.

Two of Bob's favorite web sites for doing research on almost any topic are:

- www.refdesk.com, and

- www.northernlight.com.

First, let's question how, by being an information resource, you can enhance your NetWeaving skills and your worth to all those with whom you come into contact.

The Internet has helped create a world where information, on practically any topic, has become a commodity. You've probably heard the saying—"Knowledge is power!" Today, the same can be said of information in general—access to information is power! In the past, only the privileged minority had access to much of the most critical information and, as a consequence of their access, they were considered experts. Now, expert information is available to *all*, at least to those who know where it is and how to find it.

An Internet Los Alamos

To put things in perspective, think about what happened back in the '40s during WWII when the top scientists in the U.S. were assembled at Los Alamos, New Mexico. They were told, "Look, you guys eat, sleep and drink together and don't come out until you find a way to make The Bomb." Every morning, that group of geniuses awoke knowing exactly what they had accomplished the day before and what they were going to do that day in order to correct what didn't work the previous day. Had they been in separate locations, those scientists certainly could have talked but it would have been mostly one-on-one and much of it would have been lost or misinterpreted. Regardless of what you think about the Manhattan Project, there is no question that it never would have been accomplished had it not been for the in-person cooperative effort.

Consider what the Internet represents. Every morning scientists, researchers, stock market and economic analysts awaken and have immediate access to what the brightest minds in their specific field did the previous day, what they did to correct or overcome what didn't work, or to ascertain what new revelations and discoveries others in their field have made.

Every citizen has access to much of the same information. The only roadblock to having the same access as the experts is determining how to obtain it and then finding the time to sift through all the data to pinpoint the details.

Guess what? Your prospects and clients are in the same boat. Some of them are brilliant and have already plugged into the Internet. They are tracking everything from their stocks and investments to economic data for their businesses thereby providing themselves with an early warning about any market swing information. When or if their schedules are too full, they have a staff that will do the filtering for them. Most, however, especially those who have consciously missed the computer revolution and are proud of it, are at a distinct competitive disadvantage.

We are not suggesting that you become an expert in all fields, but rather that you focus on those segments of your particular industry and those of your target client niches. For example, here is a sampling of some sites that you might focus on if you are involved in the investment side of the financial services business.

- www.barrons.com: *Barrons* magazine.

- www.bigcharts.com: Enter the company name or symbol and the program will chart the historical performance of the company's stock.

- www.businessweek.com: Online *Business Week* magazine.

- www.cdc.gov: The Center for Disease Control.

- www.cnnfn.com: CNN financial news.

- www.dbc.com: Provides a wide array of investment information.

- www.fedworld.gov: Gives you an index of all federal government agencies and information sources.

- www.hoovers.com: This is a subscription service with good information.

- www.irs.com: An excellent source for all kinds of information.

- www.micropal: Is a first-rate information source on funds with good teaching tools.

- www.morningstar.com: Has a wide variety of investment data.

- www.pcquote.com: Has a good range of facts and figures and also links to www.quote.com, an excellent source for a summation of investment news.

- www.quotesmith.com: Another great source for knowledge regarding a number of financial services products.

- www.schwab.com: One of several discount brokerage sites.

- www.sec.gov/edgarhp.htm: Corporate filings to the Securities and Exchange Commission.

- www.wsj.com: The *Wall Street Journal* site that includes the ability to subscribe on-line and then filter the information by personalizing your own home page with only those sections you choose to read.

Remember, it's not so much that you must visit every one of these sites on a regular basis, but you can recommend them to your clients as a resource when they need help in a business, family or personal context.

What It Means to Be a Resource Provider

During conversations with your clients, if you are listening closely, you will pick up opportunities for you to NetWeave as a resource provider. Here is a good example.

Gary Williams and Jeff Scroggin, both of whom were mentioned in previous chapters, are great friends and mutual NetWeavers. Gary and Jeff met years ago and have always kept in touch by getting together for an occasional breakfast or lunch to catch up with each other both personally as well as professionally. As Jeff noted, "Gary seems to know more people than almost anyone I know." Jeff has been the beneficiary of many of those contacts.

In one recent instance, their conversation had nothing to do with business. During lunch Jeff made the comment that his son was thinking of going to college in North Carolina. Gary indicated that a friend of his was on the board of directors of the particular college and that when he returned to his office he would call Jeff and give him the man's home phone number. After some phone tag, Gary's friend, a retired executive, and Jeff talked about the school, the man's current involvement in the school and where the school was headed. The conversation also included a personal commitment by the board member regarding the program about which Jeff's son was most interested.

About 45 minutes later, while Jeff was on the telephone with a client, his secretary interrupted him with a note that indicated the president of the college in which Jeff's son was interested was on the other line. Jeff concluded his initial call then spoke with the college's president about his son's admission and his fascination with the particular program.

While the president was reviewing the younger Scroggin's file, he noticed that Jeff was an attorney and asked about the kind of law he practiced. When Jeff replied that he was a tax lawyer, the two of them engaged in discussing possible ways Jeff could help the college in the area of planned giving, a primary area of Jeff's practice.

That account is not only a great example of NetWeaving in a personal context, but it is also a noteworthy case study of the NetWeaver's Quilt and how the connections can take many different twists and turns, many of which are totally unforeseen.

In Jeff's case, the story wasn't over. A few days after his conversation with the college president, Jeff was talking with a long-time client and mentioned that his son was considering attending the college in North Carolina. Jeff went on to relate how he was trying to attend an open house that was scheduled for the spring but was having a difficult time finding a hotel room. The client proceeded to offer Jeff and his son the use of her condominium which was located outside the city.

A few days after that conversation, Jeff made contact with an old high school friend whom he had not been in touch with for thirty years. She remarked that she was remarrying and moving to the same city in which Jeff's son's college was located. Additionally, since her husband was going to be connected with the school, she volunteered to keep an eye on Jeff's son and provide, in a sense, a second home.

All of these events were triggered from a conversation over a lunch with a great NetWeaver.

Building a NetWeaving reputation as a reliable source of valuable information takes years to achieve. Once the reputation is established, though, it becomes a permanent asset worth more than you can imagine; it stays that way as long as the resource provider stays current.

When Others Identify You as
A Resource, Life Is Good

Whether it's a center of influence, a charitable institution, a university or a reporter or editor with some publication, once you establish yourself as a reliable resource provider, most of your prospecting days are over.

Tom Rogerson, vice president with State Street Global Advisors, is one of the most enthusiastic and energetic people you will ever meet. He's also one of those rare individuals who can take any complex idea and reduce it to its lowest common denominator, thereby making it understandable to almost everyone. He has perfected his unique version of NetWeaving as a resource provider to such an extent that all he is required to do is show up wherever and whenever people ask him to speak. Last year alone it was 138 days.

Tom's secret as a speaker is that if you can create a message that is viewed as having genuine value, you will be placed in front of others to broadcast the message or idea. As Tom stresses, those seminars must be informational and educational and not be disguised in order to pitch a product. When he creates seminars for institutions such as Harvard University, Tom is not just invited to speak to the group. Additionally, they see his non-self-serving, educational messages as being so powerful that they position him one-on-one with some of their best benefactors.

That scenario has been repeated with engagements in front of such groups as the Young President's Organization (YPO) and even more so with the World President's Organization (WPO) where Tom is helping families of wealth come to grips with issues other than just preserving assets. Instead, he is addressing how to preserve the family assets which might often be more character assets than financial assets.

A consummate NetWeaver creates cheerleaders who do all the promoting the NetWeaver can handle. By that measure, Tom Rogerson has assembled an all-star cheerleading squad.

Helping Clients and Prospects Brainstorm

Sometimes the NetWeaver can simply help with the brain-storming process for any new idea by simply serving as a sounding board for the client or prospect. Some of the best ideas are those that are just slightly different versions of an idea that didn't work or that didn't reach its full potential. By bringing in an entirely new perspective, a new set of ideas and approaches can be generated.

Also, the NetWeaver may be able to help the person with the idea or opportunity see through some blind spots which he or she can't see or won't admit to seeing. That process can help them avoid making a major strategic mistake.

Today there are more and more companies that are being positioned as "strategic innovation" facilitators. They recognize that just as seeds germinate best when the conditions are right and the soil is properly tilled, prepared, fertilized and watered, so it is with strategic innovation. Often, companies (including many of your clients) are so caught up in the day-to-day crises that they do not take the time to just kick back and think with the brakes off the way they should. Today's new breed of idea companies creates the conditions under which innovation can be stimulated and nurtured.

One such company we have noticed that has provided quality work across numerous industries, including financial services, is IdeaScope Associates, based in Boston and San Francisco. Led by Ron Kubinski, an ex-3Mer (a company long renowned for innovative thinkers), IdeaScope has launched the Strategic Innovation Network. Drawing on IdeaScope's 18-year heritage, this exclusive forum is dedicated to the cutting-edge issues currently shaping the future of growth strategy and innovation.

IdeaScope promotes both elements of NetWeaving—providing strategic resources and strategic matchmaking. By putting together a network of members that includes strategists, innovators, visionaries, academics, venture capitalists and business leaders from around the world, and then sharing their combined talents and wisdom, IdeaScope is acting as an idea incubator.

If you have clients who wish to add ideas or expertise to their network or their newsletter, or just keep them in their NetWeaver's resource history, contact IdeaScope at <u>sinetwork@ideascope.com</u>.

The Value of Being an Information or Resource Provider

It's often said in Atlanta that if Clark Howard ever ran for mayor, he'd win—hands down. Clark Howard is a radio talk show host whose daily program on consumer money matters has one of the most loyal followings and largest audiences of any show in the country. Clark started out on the collection side of the financial services business then quit to start a travel agency. That business grew large and profitable enough that a major company acquired it. Clark had literally retired in his 30s and, together with his rental properties, could have lived comfortably without ever having to work again. One day, Clark was asked to fill in as a guest host on a radio show that dealt with travel. After hosting the program several times and getting rave reviews, he was offered his own show on which he began to touch on broad financial issues along with the travel information.

Today, Clark's show covers a variety of topics from consumer ripoffs or long distance telephone carrier comparisons to insurance issues and mortgages, just to name a few. He also gives tips on the best travel deals. If there's such a thing as a poster child for the value of being a veritable walking, talking encyclopedia of information, it's Clark.

He's translated his knowledge and experience, as well as the knowledge and experience of his great support staff who help him stay on top of virtually any topic, into an information empire. In addition to the radio show, Clark writes a regular newspaper column in the Atlanta *Journal Constitution* as well as appearing on TV.

Those who regularly listen to Clark's show are building up their own reservoirs of knowledge. That's why we say that NetWeaving is also like mentoring. You need to find mentors who will help you become a better resource to your clients and prospects.

Russ Prince, principal of Prince and Associates, is one of those phenoms within the financial services industry who has managed to carve out a niche similar to that of Clark Howard. Some think he's a clinical or behavioral psychologist; others believe he's a statistical demographic researcher. Russ is all of those plus a strategic coach and best practices advisor to high end producers, planners and advisors, as well as to high net worth individuals.

His unique style of NetWeaving comes not just from being known as a valuable strategic resource, but more importantly from being someone who interacts with many of the most successful people in the financial services industry. By learning what they do to be so successful, Russ is able to share those secrets with others. The art that Russ brings to NetWeaving lies in being able to filter through all the possible strategies and practices that *could* be applied in a certain situation and, in his words, acting as a "funnel to condense the noise" so that what comes out is an individualized set of recommendations that are best suited to that individual's personality and business model.

Russ's approach would make a great academic model for what a graduate level course in NetWeaving as a strategic resource might look like. Although few would probably graduate with honors, Russ's organization has numerous consultants, most of whom Russ has mentored and trained in his style and approach. His approach to teaching proves that many of the talents and skills are transferable.

A NetWeaver who specializes within a specific industry and who is able to attract some of the most visibly successful individuals to his stable of clients, can bring some of those same shared best practices to the table of other clients. That ability will increase your own value as a strategic resource.

Being a Resource of Topics

In the early days of Bob's insurance career he, like many agents, sent out a newsletter to clients and centers of influence on the usual tax and financial planning topics. What he found was that few of them were actually being read and even then, there was not a direct association between the newsletter and myself.

Although at the time Bob was still servicing a several hundred person client base, he was actually performing a marketing role inside the life insurance company. As a consequence of that position, he was receiving a health and fitness newsletter from Employer's Reinsurance Company (ERC). All the articles were short, concise and interesting and included selected portions of articles from a number of other health and fitness newsletters; it was a best of the best in health and fitness news.

Bob liked the newsletter so much that he called Employer's Reinsurance Company to ask if he could buy some extra copies on which he would rubber stamp his name and address under ERC's name. That's when it became interesting. Out of the blue, Bob began to receive calls from people thanking him for sending the newsletter. Many would also ask for permission to put some of the articles in their company newsletter. In addition, along with that call of thanks, there was an, "Oh, by the way, I've been thinking that we probably need to review some of my insurance needs." That had never happened to Bob before.

By the time Bob moved to Atlanta in 1981, he was sending out several hundred health and fitness newsletters. He called ERC to ask if they would just sell him the information and permit him to distribute a private label version on his own. To Bob's amazement, he was told, "We don't write it. A man in Atlanta writes it and we just put our name on it." Now living in Atlanta, Bob called the individual to discuss his idea. Not only did Bob create his own version, but he referred to the newsletter's creator dozens of other agents and planners who now distribute copies themselves.

Today, Bob writes a cover letter that he sends out every other month along with the newsletter. There is never a month that something good does not come about because of the mailing, either in the form of more business, a call of appreciation or a suggestion to call someone who has seen the newsletter.

Industry Experts Are Especially Well Positioned to Be Great NetWeavers

Someone else who epitomizes the virtues of being a walking encyclopedia in the insurance business is Hank George. If there's a more voracious reader and student of medical literature than Hank, I'd like to know who it is. Hank is a resource who freely shares his expertise with all those who seek him out

Hank, who spends most of his time on the road speaking and acting as a goodwill ambassador for LabOne, his employer, has helped a number of insurance brokers over the years as a NetWeaving resource. On one of those occasions, Hank was contacted by a broker whose brother had been declined for insurance based upon "elevated liver enzymes." The concern of the broker was less about insurance and more about the health status of his brother, whose own physician was seemingly unconcerned with the insurer's decision to deny coverage. The physician even told the broker's brother there was nothing to worry about!

Hank volunteered to review the test results which were actually sent to a lab other than the one Hank represented (and from which the broker had properly secured the test results on his brother's behalf). Hank took one look at the results and recommended that the broker ask his brother some very focused questions about his medical history and, particularly, about his family medical history. It turned out that Hank's intuition had been correct and after he saw the family history, he urged the broker to have his brother take two additional lab tests immediately.

Those tests confirmed a diagnosis of hereditary hemochromatosis and his brother began to receive periodic phlebotomies [blood draws] before there was any significant sign of iron buildup in his internal organs. Left untreated, that condition would have eventually caused irreversible damage. For the insurance broker, not only had he possibly saved his brother's life by acting as a NetWeaving resource (through Hank) but, within a year, he was able to secure for his brother a standard rating for insurance where only a year before his brother had been declined. Hank was a hero to both the broker and his brother.

Another good example of someone who is in the health and fitness business and who is a resource for a NetWeaver (Bob has used him) is Lew Schiffman. Lew, president of Atlanta Health Systems, "walks the walk" when it comes to health, fitness and nutrition. One day as Lew was working out at a fitness center, he began talking with a fellow who told him how exercising had proven to be the only way he could deal with the insomnia and stomach problems that had troubled him for years, largely due to the stress of owning and running his own company.

Lew gave him some tips and suggestions on how to confront his problems and stayed in touch. Eventually, the man showed his gratitude by hiring Lew as his personal coach. That relationship proved so successful that the man brought in Lew to work with his company's employees on conflict resolution. Lew even made recommendations that enabled the owner to discharge a person who had been a source of great stress to the whole organization.

The company has since grown dramatically and moved into larger quarters. The owner's son has since gone into the business and Lew continues to work with the next generation.

Remember, sometimes NetWeaving can be nothing more than being a helpful resource in a personal situation which then morphs into a business one.

Remember You Don't Need to Be the Expert Yourself

When financial services professionals are asked why they are not doing more "resource providing" for their clients and prospects, a common response is, "I don't consider myself to be an *expert* in that area and would be uncomfortable holding myself out as such."

Today, between the Internet and companies that are positioning themselves as distance knowledge experts, you can become a virtual expert in areas you might not have even approached before.

One company that is a pioneer in that area is Magner Financial in Atlanta, Georgia (www.magner.net). Rich Magner and Steve Roy, J.D., previously ran the large case COLI (Corporate Owned Life Insurance) operation for CIGNA; they also placed the first private placement variable life policy in the U.S. By assembling industry experts in a number of areas (human resources, executive disability, international benefits, private placement variable universal life, stock options), in addition to their own expertise in the deferred compensation area, and transferring that knowledge into user-friendly retrieval web-based systems, they enabled agents, planners and advisors to personally handle sophisticated cases that they had been either ignoring or referring to others.

In Bob's opinion, Rich and Steve have cracked the code for opening up the superaffluent market of those who own and operate small and medium-sized businesses in the area of nonqualified deferred compensation. They are achieving success by putting the expertise on the Internet as well as by bringing the client into the administration triangle where they can access and update important information whenever they want. That process helps make those plans manageable and affordable.

Yet, Rich and Steve's sights are set on the upper end of the affluent market, whether it's a business or just a single, wealthy individual. They put themselves in the shoes of the superaffluent and look at those products and services that could be of great interest to them. By then building the tools that allows agents, planners and advisors to solve the clients' needs, Magner offerings have become a virtual NetWeaver's resource provider.

Other Members of the NetWeaver's Resource Team

The financial services sector is changing character rapidly and clients are finding that the best advisors are providing them with services and resources that are far beyond the realm of the limited world they used to provide.

Several years ago, one of the missing services became very obvious to Bob Littell, mostly as a result of being a co-creator of *The Family Incentive Trust*, a planning tool designed to deal with most estate owners' desire to transfer character incentives, rather than just assets, as part of the legacy they would leave to future generations.

What he and co-creator, Jeff Scroggin, noticed was that many of the estate and financial planning issues being considered, or which had already been put in place, would probably either never be implemented or would blowup somewhere down the line. That would happen because all the advisors either ignored or never bothered to look into or flush out some significant dysfunctional family and or business problems. Today, a growing number of family business succession planning firms focus *first* on those issues and put the planning second. Often, these advisors bring in, or have on staff, clinical psychologists who help bring these issues out in the open where they can be discussed and often resolved.

In addition to adding a clinical psychologist or two as resources in your NetWeaver's resource file, there are a host of other services that will become much more common in the future.

Business planning strategists and facilitators will be but one of many new and important resources that the best NetWeaving agents, planners and advisors will be adding to their resource directories in the years to come.

Riding the Aging Wave

Another area that crosses both the family and personal contexts, and sometimes the business context as it relates to a family owned business, concerns our aging society. Today there are 4.3 million people age 85 and older and many of them will live into their 90s, some even past 100. That age group represents the fastest growing segment of society, not only in the U.S. but in most of the industrialized nations. Over the next ten years, the number of individuals age 85 or older will increase by about 1.5 million.

In many of those situations, there will be some form of care required and yet few adult children with aging parents are prepared for the consequences of handling all the associated issues. Not only that, but those same adult children of needy parents must face up to the fact that one day, assuming they live that long, they will face many of the same issues.

Literally thousands of products and services will be needed to accommodate this age boom from medical supplies, appliances and medications to products and services focused around keeping people active as long as possible—both physically as well as mentally.

Every person in the financial services industry can become a better NetWeaving resource by becoming more aware of and knowledgeable about the issues surrounding that segment of society. It is not only important to provide service to others but to also be in a better position to help members of our own families and, later on, ourselves.

Imagine this scenario: a top-notch, financial services power NetWeaver receives a call from a client who has questions about investments, insurance and planning related issues concerning her

85-year old mother who has just been diagnosed with early Alzheimer's disease. How would this professional handle the situation? She would:

- Become familiar with the different levels of care in the community; especially with some of the non-profit caregiver organizations that provide valuable counseling or support services. She would try to match someone in one of those organizations with the client's mother or another family member.

- Learn the basics of long-term care insurance and the world of new definitions: "Activities of Daily Living" (ADL) such as eating, bathing, dressing, toileting, etc.; "Instrumental Activities of Daily Living" (IADLs) like shopping or doing housework, etc.; "Independent Living" or "Assisted Living Skilled Care" and more. That information could then be sent to the client. Moreover, the client could be sent an invitation to a long-term care lecture or seminar where she might possibly connect with the speaker as a resource.

- Have at least a working knowledge of the basic planning tools: Medical Power of Attorney, the Living Will, the provisions of Medicare and what Medicaid does and does not cover.

- Surf the Internet for whatever resources are available, for example:

  - www.aarp.org,

  - www.seniornet.com,

  - www.elderhostel.org and

  - www.mentalhealth.about.com.

There are so many resources available that the professional power NetWeaver must know how to find them. Your clients and prospects will consider those resources to be of tremendous value.

NetWeavers Make the Best Mentors

Almost without exception, show us a skilled NetWeaver, either as a strategic matchmaker or as a gifted resource provider, and we'll show you someone who passes those skills on to others. NetWeavers tend to be people who enjoy mentoring other people. Just as NetWeaving involves putting *other* people together in win/win relationships, that is usually a sign that those individuals enjoy helping other people become successful.

Few people in the insurance industry are better known as a mentor and NetWeaver than B.B. Brown, past president of the Society of Financial Service Professionals. Yet, B.B. would be the first to tell you that he is simply passing on the baton that was handed to him by those who came before.

As a mentor and matchmaker, B.B. remembers John "Johnny" B. Jackson Jr. as one of his greatest NetWeaver role models. He recalled Johnny's insatiable sense of curiosity as well as his desire to share with all his friends anything he found worthwhile.

Most who know B.B. would call him a dapper dresser, but B.B. points out that wasn't always the case. When B.B. entered the life insurance business, he had a few suits that probably reflected the tastes of the clothing salesmen who had sold them to him. Johnny was a few years older than B.B. and already an established agent. One day Johnny said, "Brown, you are going to buy another suit one of these days, and I want to help you." At that time, B.B. hadn't been married long but he had a new baby, an old car and a new agent's income; he hadn't even given a second thought to buying a new suit. But Johnny clearly wanted to help so B.B.went along with the idea.

The year was 1952 and Johnny explained that suits should have a natural shoulder, three buttons, no darts and no pleats in the trousers. He took B.B. to a hotel where the traveling representative of Brooks Brothers had a trunk show. Johnny instructed B.B. to pick a conservative fabric from a swatch book and then get measured. For $85.00, B.B ordered his first custom made suit. Johnny picked out a couple of white cotton oxford button down shirts and two regimental ties that complemented the suit fabric. "Well, that's a start," Johnny said to the stunned BB, and it was also just a start to a mentoring relationship that lasted for over forty years. Whenever Johnny discovered something he thought was good, he shared it with his many friends.

His advice was usually very good, but his friends still laugh about the one time when his advice wasn't so good. Just after World War II, Atlanta was a hub of Naval Reserve activity. Young officers joined units that met one night a week and very few of those units had cherished pay billets. Johnny discovered a new unit that was forming and quickly persuaded some of his closest friends to join so they could get into the pay billets. The unit was then ordered to active duty during the Korean War. Johnny was sent to the Pentagon where he and his young bride enjoyed two years in Washington, D.C.; his friends were not so lucky. One went to French West Africa, another to Guam and a third to an obscure naval base in Japan.

Johnny died some years ago, but his memory is still alive. Whenever any two of his friends meet they always end up swapping "Jackson stories" about his many exploits, many of which involved some form of NetWeaving. B.B. pointed out that Johnny was always willing to share with others—how to do better in life—and that characteristic is a sure sign of a great NetWeaver.

The story about Johnny and B.B. also illustrates that very simple acts of NetWeaving can often have an impact down the road that is totally unforeseen but which will leave a lasting and significant impression.

LaDale Young, as previously mentioned in Chapter 8, is one of those rare NetWeavers who actually gets more pleasure out of being on the giving end rather than on the receiving end. "I just get this really great feeling after I've put two people together and something good happens," remarks LaDale, "or when I refer an individual to someone in my network of resources when I know they're going to be treated right, whether it's buying a car or a pair of shoes."

And LaDale knows his shoes. When he was in college, LaDale worked his way through school by working multiple jobs with crazy hours. One of those jobs was as a representative for a top of the line shoe manufacturer. Early on he learned to advance himself by getting his friends to spread the word among the fraternity and sorority houses that he would be stopping by on a certain day with a new shipment of shoes. LaDale built his business by becoming a convenient "shoe resource."

To illustrate how going that one extra step often pays off, LaDale took a tennis course for two semesters from Coach Murdock. One day LaDale wore a pair of very attractive alligator saddle oxfords about which the coach remarked how great they looked. LaDale told the coach he would get him a pair and quoted him a price of $90 with tax. On a coach's salary (probably around $7,500 a year) back in the 1960s, that was a huge amount of money. To close the deal, LaDale even let the coach pay for the shoes over time.

When they ran into each other years later, Coach Murdock confided to LaDale how much his act of generosity had meant to him and his self-esteem at having those beautiful shoes. He went on to relate how he coached basketball games on the side for $10 a game and that he set aside $6 or $7 from each game to pay for the shoes. He remembered that he coached eighteen games in order to pay for the shoes.

LaDale has mentored about as many agents as anyone in the insurance industry. It is his desire to see other people succeed and improve themselves which marries so well with his NetWeaving prowess.

One of the most successful individuals we know of in the worksite marketing area is a gentleman named Hervey Ross. If ever there was a true life, walking, talking Sergeant Bilko or Cpl. Klinger (in every good sense of the word), it's Hervey. In fact, although he only attained the rank of E-3 in the Army, Hervey was one of those "go to" people who, when you needed something, especially if it fell a little bit outside the ordinary, you called Hervey. He became irreplaceable by becoming a resource provider extraordinaire.

Hervey has carried that same "make yourself an irreplaceable resource" theme into his insurance practice. He attributes the tremendous success he's enjoyed over his career to that ability. Whether it's helping people find jobs or just bringing friends, business contacts or Toastmasters Club members together in order to locate a good attorney, doctor, church or just a great restaurant, Hervey is a master matchmaker. Hervey also has been instrumental in mentoring and personally funding scholarships for students to attend Worcester Academy in Massachusetts where he sits on the board. He also mentors several young salesmen who are leading their company in sales.

Hervey simply sees his NetWeaving as a way to demonstrate his value in a manner that goes far beyond someone simply selling insurance. His rewards are commensurate with someone who adds value to so many different people's lives.

Mentoring is actually another form of NetWeaving in that the mentor is making himself available to another as a resource with no agenda other than wanting to help someone by sharing his wisdom and experience. Houston Smith, mentioned in Chapter 3 in "The Psychology of NetWeaving," is probably best known within the accounting circle for his generous mentoring activities. He has probably mentored as many young CPAs as anyone in the country. In one situation, Houston served as a mentor for a CPA who approached him to put together a financial plan for her aging parents. She did not feel comfortable (nor did her parents) sharing that detailed financial information and their feelings about the situation with others.

The CPA warned Houston that, although her parents got along well, they had tremendous arguments when it came to discussing money issues. It seemed that her father had worked his way up the company ladder virtually from stock clerk to president and, with a seven figure income, felt obligated to tithe to various charities and organizations. That was something he didn't want to discuss with his wife.

Houston was able to get the issues out on the table so both of them could openly express their thoughts and feelings. When the CPA's mother realized what her husband was doing and why, she also realized she would still be left in a very comfortable position if anything was to happen to him. At that point, Houston said he could literally see the tension between them disappear before his eyes.

chapter

11

SUMMARY

"A man may die, nations may rise and fall, but an idea lives on."

— JOHN F. KENNEDY

As we hope you recognize after reading this book, although NetWeaving™ certainly involves strategies and techniques that can be developed or improved upon, it's really more about a great way to live your life—both personally and professionally. To be constantly on the lookout for ways to put people together in fortuitous relationships and to strive to become a resource for others—either through yourself or by offering your extended NetWeaver's resource bank—that is truly a great feeling. As a NetWeaver, you become more effective for everyone you serve whether that means your clients, your prospects, your family or any charitable organizations with which you are involved.

Since NetWeaving sets up the possibility for *future* sales of products and services for those in the financial services industry, this book was not written with the idea of developing a specific set of sales tips. If you become a talented NetWeaver, as we have shown is possible through all of the stories and case studies, the income part of the formula will take care of itself. Good things really do happen to people who *make* good things happen. In fact, as several of the most successful NetWeavers in this book have observed, they are amazed that other people don't do more of it or do it more often.

If you accept the role of NetWeaver, you must be willing to trust the process and have the confidence to know that your benevolence will pay off in the long run. At the same time, you must be up front with the mindset and attitude to genuinely feel that a payoff is not why you became a NetWeaver.

You must also be willing to take risks. Some relationships you help set up will not work out. Some resources that you provide will not prove as effective or helpful as you had originally believed. That's life.

Recipients of a NetWeaver's bounty and generosity seldom blame the matchmaker or the resource provider if the relationship does not perform as expected. Further, I'm reminded of Mark Schooler's phrase in Chapter 3: "My purpose in getting the two of you together is for you to gain a better understanding of how each of you make money. After you both understand that, and determine if you have anything in common or if you can be of help to each other, the rest is up to you."

Nevertheless, that fear of potentially being held responsible for a relationship that doesn't work out, or a resource that doesn't fulfill its potential, is, unfortunately, going to keep many individuals from ever realizing the rewards and joys of NetWeaving.

Anyone who still has doubts about the advantages of NetWeaving over more inwardly focused brands of networking should talk with Stanley Zimmerman, former president of the Mortgage Institute of California as well as president of the National Home Equity Association, and currently president of Home Budget Loans in Los Angeles, California. Stanley also serves as a commissioner on the State of California Little Hoover Commission.

Stanley says that in the early years of running his company he took it very personally when an employee of his resigned in order to start a new business in competition with him. He said he would often do everything in his power to make it difficult for that person to be successful.

Somewhere along the way he realized that method wasn't working and decided to try the opposite approach; he would help his new "competitor" get started. Acting sometimes as a strategic matchmaker and other times helping provide strategic resources to the competition he now supported, Stanley not only maintained a friendly relationship that paid off in many ways, but it brought him more business, not less.

The negative energies involved in negative activities almost always lose in comparison to positive energies applied under the same set of circumstances. NetWeaving is all about bringing positive energy into relationships.

For those with the courage to NetWeave, the course is simple: build your NetWeaver's resource base—information and contacts.

Build the habits of listening differently; share the NetWeaver's philosophy with others and watch how they respond. Go out and NetWeave every single day. Not only will your success far exceed anything you have ever dreamed but one day, as you sit back and review your life and your career, your NetWeaving episodes and experiences will be your most memorable and rewarding. Good NetWeaving!

appendix

THE 10 STRATEGIC CONCEPTS TO POWER NETWEAVING

1. Always be on the lookout for NetWeaving™ opportunities—they are everywhere. Train yourself how to watch, listen and recognize those opportunities.

2. Act as if *everyone's* problems are *your* problems and *everyone's* opportunities are *your* opportunities. Learn to walk in their moccasins.

3. Become a good jigsaw puzzle player. In other words, always look for ways to fill in more empty spaces of your Global Stepping-Stone chain.

4. Be genuine and sincere in your power NetWeaving by having the confidence to know that your matchmaking will come back to benefit you in many ways in the future. You do not need to ask for anything up front; your reward will come.

5. Be creative in helping prospects and clients find ways to solve their problems and ways to take advantage of their opportunities. Associate with off-the-wall thinkers, especially if that's not your strong suit. Challenge the status quo and "the way things have always been done." Wild-eyed brainstorming, with the brakes off, creates opportunities that most people walk by everyday but miss.

6. Become a well-rounded reader. Use consolidated services such as the *Kiplinger Letter*, *Bottom Line*, *Financial Services Online* or *Executive Book Summaries* (summaries of business books and articles). Also look to your local business journal.

7. Always be on the lookout for a "charitable twist"—a way to perform good deeds that results in favorable publicity for your client's business. Use word-of-mouth promotion.

8. Accept the fact that NetWeaving is a learned behavior that takes practice and more practice. It's not a natural activity for most people. Make a daily habit of it.

9.   Spread the word about the effectiveness of NetWeaving. The more NetWeavers there are, the better it is for *all* of us. You'll get the credit for being a NetWeaving pioneer.

10. Remember that power NetWeaving is just following the Golden Rule: "Do unto others as you would have them do unto you."

appendix

B

NetWeaving
Tracking Systems

Several times in this book, we suggested that you store your NetWeaving™ resources—people, information, products, services, etc.—in your mental Rolodex for later retrieval. For many of us, especially those of us who seem to have more "senior moments" than we did in days gone by, depending on our memory is a recipe for disaster. Therefore, you must have a good system for storing your resource information for quick retrieval if you are going to become a power NetWeaver.

We do not have a specific recommendation as to whether your system should be a manual, paper-based method or one that is based upon today's computer technology. You must decide for yourself which method is most comfortable and easiest for you to use.

Whichever method you decide on, you might want to consider the approach outlined below. It is a clean, easy to use and adaptable example that allows you to put your hands on the information you need quickly while providing you with the necessary detail.

Strategic NetWeaving Resource File

RESOURCE PROVIDING NETWEAVING CATEGORIES:

1. Person with a need.
2. Person with a product or service.
3. Person with a problem.
4. Person with a solution.

6. Person with an idea or opportunity.
7. Person who can enhance or facilitate an idea.
8. Acting as a resource provider yourself.
9. Another person acting as a resource provider.

CONTEXT
- Business
- Family
- Personal

NAME	TELEPHONE	E-MAIL ADDRESS	RESOURCE CATEGORY
John Jones clinical psychologist specializing in family-owned businesses	404-333-3333	jsj@urthere.com	2
Myself excellent general reference	Myself	www.refdesk.com	7
Bill Johnson creative advertising/ marketing	555-749-8255	billyj@ideas.com	8
Wendy Hanson designer/publisher	713-222-2222	publish@desktop	4
Terry Barry new business owner specializing in electrical products	724-987-1234	electricman@1.com	1

.